BILLION DOLLAR HOLLYWOOD HEIST

THE A-LIST KINGPIN AND THE POKER RING THAT BROUGHT DOWN TINSELTOWN

HOUSTON CURTIS AND DYLAN HOWARD

Skyhorse Publishing

Skyhorse Publishing books may be purchased in bulk at special discounts for sales promotion, corporate gifts, fund-raising, or educational purposes. Special editions can also be created to specifications. For details, contact the Special Sales Department, Skyhorse Publishing, 307 West 36th Street, 11th Floor, New York, NY 10018 or info@skyhorsepublishing.com.

Skyhorse® and Skyhorse Publishing® are registered trademarks of Skyhorse Publishing, Inc.®, a Delaware corporation.

Visit our website at www.skyhorsepublishing.com.

10 9 8 7 6 5 4 3

Library of Congress Cataloging-in-Publication Data is available on file.

Jacket design by 5mediadesign
Front jacket photos credit: BigStockPhoto
Back jacket photos courtesy of the author

Print ISBN: 978-1-5107-5507-9
Ebook ISBN: 978-1-5107-6217-6

Printed in the United States of America

To all those who stood by me in the dark as well as the light. You know who you are.

SPECIAL THANKS

To my daughters Chloe and Callie for their unconditional love, as well as the entire Curtis and Sutherland family.

Dave Weidenhoffer, Jon Moonves, Rick Mahr, Steve Pacey, and Tobey Maguire.

Ricky, Tony, Jack, Kimberly, and the entire Curtis clan for their love and help.

Norma Curtis, Mack Curtis, and the entire Sutherland family, Jimmy Carter, Jared & Jacob Carter, Darla and Dan, along with the entire Moore and Wolsefer family, Kye, Brittin, Elijah, and Preston.

Bonnie Buckley Curtis and the entire Buckley family including Brad, Lori, Andy, Nancy, Fred, and Corrine. The Pazuks, Cynthia, Katherine, Steve, and Beverly, Sam Nafisi and the Nafisi family, Alex and Tom Grane and family, Vin Di Bona, Cara and Danny Swartz and family, Liam Waite, Jason Gordon Thomas, Andrew and Maggie Crosby, Alex Avant, Natasha Henstridge, Hector Hank, Marc Teschner, Lisa Teschner, Sam and Fernanda Hurwitz, Stacia Saint Owens, Dave Weiderman, Kevin Kleinrock, Jeff Kelly, Erica Gill, Chick Alcorn, Steve Kaminski, Sam Korkis, Howard Mann, Oliver Mann, Greg Lipstone, Adam Sher, Richard

Lawrence, Seth Lawrence, Puraj Puri, Lois Curren, Brian Graden, Jeff Olde, Sarah Weidman, Burt DuBrow, Bob Banner, Phil Hellmuth, Annie Duke, Joe Reitman, Andy Bloch, Jason Hervey, Jerry Katell, Anthony Curtis, Russ Hamilton and Bob Dunbar. Morgan Nichols, John Cooksey and Matt Lindenberg.

Chad Henry, Bob Bell, Ryan Garland, Shaina Rae Barton, Guy Bale, Randy Anagnostis, and everyone at Skyhorse Publishing. The LA Poker regulars including Nick Cassavettes, Leo DiCaprio, Kasey Thompson, Rick Solomon, Kevin Washington, Todd Phillips, Darin Feinstein, Andy Bellin, Jonny Moon, Bob Safi, Mike Baxter, Dave Garden, Steve Brill, Ben Affleck, Matt Damon, Larry "Old Spice" Haun, Chuck Pacheco, Reagan Silber, Dylan Sellers, Dean Factor, Bosko, Jon Brooks, Codey Leibel, Manny Lopez, James Woods, Chris Williams, Irv Gotti, Mark Weidmen, Hank Azaria, Jamie Gold, Jon Landau, Andrew Shack, Mike Sexton, Vince Van Patten, Gabe Kaplan, Andrew Sasson, Guy Laliberte, Alec Gores, and all of the other players who made high stakes poker in Hollywood the experience of a lifetime.

Lastly, a big thanks to Dominic Utton and Dylan Howard.

TABLE OF CONTENTS

INTRODUCTION
BY DYLAN HOWARD

A powerful man like Bradley Ruderman rarely answered his office phone. But on this occasion, the multimillionaire hedge fund manager picked up. Just as well. When the caller identified himself, Ruderman was taken aback. It was Tobey Maguire. *The* Tobey Maguire.

Ruderman was used to mixing with the rich and influential; his hedge fund managed millions of dollars of other people's money from offices in Beverly Hills. This, though, was different. Maguire was Hollywood A-list. And there was more. An intriguing invitation, extended to him: "He said, 'Hey, we have this game . . . Would you like to play?'"

Spider-Man was asking him round to his house to play poker.

Now, for the first time, this book can reveal exclusively the exact details of how Ruderman—who served time in a Texas prison after being convicted of embezzling $25 million from his investors—was drawn into a clandestine world of high-stakes illegal poker games, a secret society that included Ben Affleck, Matt Damon, and Leonardo DiCaprio as some of its most noted alumni.

It was a story that was to end in multimillion-dollar fraud, jail, and violence. One that has no heroes, but plenty of victims. Today Ruderman—a mini-Madoff—has every reason to bitterly regret taking the call that fateful day in 2006. But Maguire will almost certainly wish he never made it.

Ruderman's tale was documented in a 206-page deposition that was conducted on March 29 at Taft Community Correctional Facility in Kern County, California. As one of the foremost investigative journalists in Hollywood, I exclusively obtained the transcript of that interrogation. Using Ruderman's words, I was able to tell the full story of Hollywood's high-roller card sharks for the first time.

His videotaped testimony, on oath and under the penalty of perjury, tells the explosive tale of his fall from grace, beginning in 2006 when he was still chief executive of Ruderman Capital Partners.

It was not, however, Maguire's call that began the sad case of a man corrupted by the twinkling lights of fame and danger. That came a few weeks earlier, after Ruderman was walking along the pristine Pacific Ocean coastline in Malibu.

Ruderman, then in his early forties, was strolling on Carbon Beach—the star-studded enclave of the rich and famous—when he bumped into a friend who was at a barbecue on the sand. It was no ordinary family barbecue. The host was Rick Salomon, otherwise known as Paris Hilton's infamous sex-tape partner.

At the party, Ruderman got talking to a beautiful brunette. She was thirty-three-year-old Molly Bloom, the sister of two-time Olympic skier and Philadelphia Eagles player Jeremy Bloom.

"She asked me if I would be interested in playing in a game that they were coincidentally having the following night at that house," Ruderman told lawyers in the deposition, "and she asked if I would be interested in participating, and I said, sure."

Ruderman needed little convincing. "She just told me it was a traditional Texas Hold'em game . . . that if I enjoyed gambling and enjoyed 'action' that it would be worth my while to come. I figured, you know, why not? I have nothing else to do that night and I certainly love to gamble, and it was close and it made for an easy scenario."

He was in.

The call from Maguire, whom Ruderman had never previously met, confirmed the hedge fund manager's place on the secret card circuit. Ruderman recalls in the deposition: "He had mentioned that he knew that I had played in a prior game that Molly had organized, and asked if I liked it, and I said yes.

"He says, well, that's good because we actually have a regular game that she organizes," he continued. "It's not on the beach, it's in town, and here's the facts about it and would I be interested, and I said yes." That game, it turned out, was at Maguire's Los Angeles house that he shares with his wife, Jennifer, the daughter of Ronald Meyer, president and CEO of Universal Studios, and their two children, Ruby, 5, and three-year-old Otis.

Soon Ruderman was playing regularly, usually every other week. The routine became familiar to him. Bloom invited players by text, often mentioning when stars were expected. Ruderman said in his testimony: "She [Molly] would include into your personal text message, Dave's showing up, Tobey's showing."

Bloom's games were strictly invitation-only, to venues such as the Four Seasons, the Peninsula, the Beverly Hills Hotel, and the world-famous Viper Room on Sunset Boulevard, a venue once owned by Johnny Depp. You had to be vetted by Bloom to get in. "You had to have pedigree," said Ruderman.

By 2009, Ruderman told lawyers, he was well known on the circuit as someone who paid his debts. These were no ordinary games. Secret passwords were needed to play, and the door was sometimes manned by armed guards in bulletproof vests. Everything was laid on, even shoulder massages during games to relieve tension.

Ronald Richards, one of the lawyers questioning Ruderman in prison, noted: "Molly built a service business for herself by bringing friendly, attractive girls to serve drinks, and she provided a stable location and staff to host a game."

Ruderman said the idea that attractive girls and drinks were the reason players showed up was wrong. "The reason people show up at the game, in all due respect to Molly, is not Molly. It's the other players." Like Maguire and Co., the highest-wattage members of the circle.

But Bloom, it was said, could get whatever you needed. A source said illegal drugs would sometimes be part of the action. From whom, no one ever named. "It was known to a handful of us that one player would keep two hookers down the hall of the hotel in another room," an insider said.

"He would disappear for 30 minutes at a time, leaving the main players in the game frustrated. In reality, he was going to do blow [in a room with] two hookers." (There is no suggestion any of the people named in this story used drugs or hookers; indeed, this author has chosen not to name the individual identified by multiple sources.)

If the extras on offer were unusual, the stakes involved were mind-blowing. In fact, there was no financial limit in the secret, unlicensed Texas Hold'em games. On one occasion, a player lost $300,000 in a night.

Maguire was a winner, however, taking as much as $1 million per month over a period of three years, a source suggested. "That means he could have made up to $30 to $40 million from these games," another said.

Ruderman agreed. "Tobey Maguire is the best player and a winner," he confessed to FBI agents Jeremy Tarwater and Steve Goldman in a separate, earlier interview, according to transcripts provided to a Los Angeles court and obtained by this author.

Asked about the pot, Ruderman said in his most recent testimony: "If there are eight people playing and eight people have $50,000 in chips in front of them, then there's $400,000 potentially that's at risk at any moment because it's a no-limit game.

"I believe the highest pot I ever saw, which I was not in the hand at that time, was $950,000."

Every game, players would show up and buy in, usually for $50,000, according to Ruderman. Bloom was on hand to take the money—and her cut.

"If I lost my initial $50,000 and wanted to buy in for another $50,000, she'd hand me $50,000 in chips, and I would be in for $100,000 that night," he said. "And she would keep track of that for every player, and at the end of the night, less expenses, she would have an accounting of who owed what to whom."

Bloom would pocket around $6,400 per night, Ruderman said, (which I later learned was closer to $30k per night), but she was not the house, merely a clearing agent. The next thing she would arrange was for an assistant to pick up any money owed and deliver money won.

"She would sit in close proximity to the table with a computer typing in all the various notations," Ruderman explained.

"If you were a loser, you knew that you had lost, and you knew that in the next couple of days she would be in contact with you to write a check in an amount or amounts to the various winners of that game. And usually what would happen is you couldn't play in the next game until you made good on your debts for the prior game."

Ruderman and Bloom's A-list clientele preferred private games. Why? "It's the convenience factor of playing in a controlled environment with a stable group of people where you don't have to go into a casino, and you don't have to subject yourself to, A, getting to a casino, and, B, dealing with all the riffraff that's at a casino," Ruderman explained. "It's easy. It's user friendly and that's why I played. And, you know, on top of the fact that I was hooked."

The atmosphere was undoubtedly heady and adrenaline-laden, but there was one big problem for Brad Ruderman: he was a poor player. As Academy Award-winner Damon says at the start of the 1998 poker movie, *Rounders*: "Listen, here's the thing: if you can't spot the sucker in your first half hour at the table, then you are the sucker."

Unsurprisingly, others were delighted to have Ruderman play. "He was easy to take advantage of," said one of the game's big winners. "Ruderman was one of the biggest losers in the game. For the core group of players, having someone with deep pockets and no poker skills was a dream come true."

Ruderman eventually accepted that he was indeed the sucker. As his losses spiraled out of control, he stole more than $5.2 million from his clients to pay off his poker debts. He told the FBI that Bloom preyed on him because he was "not a good gambler." Bloom "was very aggressive to get me to keep playing," Ruderman said in a 2009 interview.

He was clearly addicted to gambling and prepared to do anything to satisfy his craving. "I was a loser," Ruderman said in the deposition. "I'm thinking like any gambler is thinking or any pathological gambler is thinking. You're not keeping track of the actual numbers. You're thinking, I'm that much closer to going on the big run. That's the juice."

In his testimony, he confessed: "I traded securities every single day. I tried to make clients' money. As it turned out, I didn't do it very well, and I misrepresented those performances figures to my clients."

"You would just literally take client money and take it out of the fund?" he was asked.

"That's why I'm here [in jail] today."

Ruderman was constantly pressed on the legality of the games during his testimony. It was a crucial question, one that was to provide an unusual twist as the story played out.

Q: "I'm just trying to establish a real obvious fact. Tobey Maguire didn't think he was breaking any laws playing poker with Brad Ruderman. Right?"

A: "I can't surmise what Tobey knew, but I wouldn't presume that, no."

Q: "I mean, you guys didn't hide—you're playing at the Beverly Hills Hotel and the Four Seasons. Right?"

A: "Correct."

Ruderman recalled players discussing whether the games were legal. Did they consult a lawyer, he was asked.

"No. I never did . . . everybody plays cards at homes. Playing cards at home is not illegal. It happens all the time. It's okay to do that . . .," he said.

"What made this different was the fact that we had Molly Bloom and she was performing a function that was, shall we say, unusual for a typical home poker game," he continued. "And so many of us at the table one night, I vividly remember this, were discussing that very fact like, Hey, you know, she's taking a piece of the action, and what's her role here?"

Some people were invited but rebuffed the group. "There were people that didn't want to play in this game because they were concerned about that."

He was instructed to name names.

"I'd rather not say, but they're very, very prominent people," said Ruderman.

"I'm going to request that you answer the question," a lawyer said.

He finally relented. "Was this person's name brought up at the table?" a lawyer asked.

"Did I bring it up?" he responded. "No. But was Jeffery Katzenberg's name brought up? Yes."

Katzenberg, CEO of DreamWorks Animation and the former chairman of Walt Disney Studios, wasn't the only big-name name checked in the deposition. Also playing were pro player Kenny Tran, Nick Cassavetes (director of *The Notebook*), and billionaire business-man Alec Gores, who once tried to buy the film studio Miramax.

But by far the most intriguing is New York Yankees slugger Alex Rodriguez—all the more so because his spokesman has long denied this author's reporting that the man known as A-Rod played in the high-stakes ring.

In his testimony, Ruderman was specifically questioned by lawyers about one particular game.

"I can give you some of the names I remember," he told the attorneys.

"Kenny Tran, Alex Rodriguez."

"The baseball player?" one lawyer asked, somewhat surprised.

"Yes," Ruderman said.

Even though a cavalcade of stars kept joining the circuit, things were souring and the atmosphere turning ugly. By 2009, Ruderman had had enough. The game was up and the chips were down.

Once his clients discovered that their savings had been squandered, an FBI investigation into the fund's finances revealed the shadowy world of the A-list gambling club. Ruderman surrendered to prosecutors in Los Angeles and confessed to bilking investors out of $25 million in a Ponzi scheme and using $5.2 million of that money to settle poker debts.

He was sentenced to 10 years in jail for two counts of wire fraud and two counts of investment adviser fraud and ordered to repay his investors, something he is unable to do.

That, though, was not the final paragraph in the story, just the end of a chapter.

Investors in his hedge fund—whose money Ruderman had taken to pay his debts—got to thinking. If the games were unlicensed and illegal, any transactions from the games were void. Investors' money handed to winning players like Maguire could be clawed back through civil suits.

This was an unexpected twist. Getting a fish like Ruderman to swim upstream had seemed a smart idea at the start. Now it didn't look so clever.

Enter Houston Curtis.

The City of Angels is full of demons stripping poor souls of their self-control, dignity, wealth—and, occasionally, their lives. From fledgling actors desperate for that one big break to Hollywood royals possessing enormous fame and fortune, Los Angeles has tragically borne witness to the demise of many. For each dreamer who has captured that coveted Hollywood ending, scores more have burned out quickly, their moment in the spotlight too elusive.

Actors, singers, and even politicians have met their demise in this unforgiving city. From Robert F. Kennedy's devastating assassination to River Phoenix's senseless overdose to Sharon Tate's brutal slaughter at the hands of the Manson Family, Los Angeles's seedier side has reared its ugly head all too many times. It has also been the scene for lighter—albeit dramatic—moments such as Hugh Grant's prostitution arrest, Rihanna's sickening beatdown at the hands of battering boyfriend Chris Brown, and Michael Richards's racist-spewing stand-up meltdown.

Houston Curtis had both. The highest of highs. And the lowest of lows.

We first met each other at a cafe on Sunset Boulevard one steamy Saturday afternoon when Houston decided to become my Deep Throat, the mysterious source who helped me break open the scandal and who has remained hidden until now. (Except for a poorly researched attempt to replicate him as Harlan Eustice, played by Bill Camp, in Aaron Sorkin's big screen adaptation of the scandal, *Molly's Game*.)

"The irony of it all is that the game finally found the biggest fish ever, Ruderman, and we did our best to bury him every week and win his millions. Now those who fleeced him of millions are embroiled in this lawsuit. It's like he turned the tables on us with no skill, just sheer stupidity," Houston told me the first time we met.

But the truth is that the real story behind *Molly's Game* has not been told—until now.

Sure, the civil cases soon found their targets. Cassavetes, Salomon, and *Welcome Back, Kotter* star Gabe Kaplan were also sued. Details soon started leaking out. It was said that Ruderman lost $311,300 to Maguire, including one losing hand of $110,000 in 2007. The actor countered by saying that his winnings only amounted to around $187,000 and insisted he lost nearly as much as he won . . . a statement that made Houston Curtis burst into uncontrollable laughter. Houston got saddled with close to a million dollars' worth of checks directly from Ruderman and claimed that he couldn't ever remember a time where Ruderman had a winning night. In fact, he couldn't remember a time when Ruderman lost less than six figures a night during the entire stretch he played in the game.

And Hollywood watchers geared themselves up for the full public hearing, where all the details would come out. But it never happened. All players in the ring did the sensible thing and settled with the exception of Houston Curtis, who ended up losing his three-million-dollar Sherman Oaks house after a $750k lien was put on it from the Ruderman scandal. In all, the twenty-two people who sued to recoup poker winnings received a total of more than $1.75 million. And according to Houston, the biggest name on the recoup list was billionaire Alec Gores, who once told Houston he had personally invested 10 million with Ruderman. Alec was on both sides, since he took checks from Ruderman in the poker game but invested in his hedge fund, as well. Aside from Curtis, whose life began turning upside down after Molly leaked his name to the feds in her cooperation with the Ruderman case, a slew of famous names eventually breathed a sigh of relief. They all settled for about 50 cents on the dollar and didn't have to appear in court.

That is why Ruderman's deposition, made before the settlement, was so important in shining a light on the underground poker ring. He insisted he was only speaking out to help the victims of his crimes, but he knew it was not without risk.

When Ruderman surrendered to FBI agents after being charged, he was concerned players would try to kill him.

One player turned up unannounced at Ruderman's home before he turned himself in. But Ruderman wouldn't open the door. "Couldn't take the chance," he said. "I had no idea if he had any other intentions in mind. At that time, I didn't know, you know, who wanted to do what to me."

Others were equally fearful. After Ruderman was arrested, Bloom left him phone messages. He told lawyers: "She said, 'Call me. We need to talk. I heard about what happened, and I have to talk to you.'"

Bloom herself relocated to New York that year to set up a new operation for Wall Street brokers. Russian mobsters are said to have joined in and violence ensued, during which Bloom was said to have been roughed up. Some insiders believe the gangsters wanted to intimidate Bloom before she was questioned by feds.

Ruderman is no angel. He defrauded people out of millions and ruined lives. But at least he had the dignity to speak out. Hollywood's A-list poker kings may have been spared the indignity of appearances in open court, but Ruderman, the man they regarded as a sucker, had the last laugh. Until now. That mantle has been handed to Houston Curtis.

PROLOGUE

They call it the "Pink Palace." For a hundred years the Beverly Hills Hotel—a discrete oasis of pure opulence off Sunset Boulevard—has played host to the cream of Hollywood and some of the richest, most famous, and most powerful men and women in the history of America, including luminaries such as the Rat Pack, Humphrey Bogart, and Marlene Dietrich. Fred Astaire read *Daily Variety* poolside, John Lennon and Yoko Ono hid out in one of the hotel's twenty-three bungalows for a week, and Richard Nixon's chief of staff learned about Watergate while eating breakfast in the famed Polo Lounge. Paramount Pictures was sold over drinks to Gulf & Western at its tables. Clark Gable was talked into acting in *The Misfits* by Arthur Miller over a tropical cocktail.

If the walls of this king and queen's castle could speak, they would whisper of a century of easy money, sex, scandal, and excess. But it's rarely seen a night like this.

We're in a luxurious bungalow at the hotel, cloistered away from the other guests, wrapped in our own private world. And whatever we want, we're getting.

There's a private butler on standby, and beautiful girls from the Ford modelling agency are giving shoulder massages for thousand-dollar tips. Nobody could agree on dinner, so we had our hostess order in food from Los Angeles's most exclusive eateries: Spago, Mastro's, and the Polo Lounge.

Leonardo DiCaprio is chilling on the couch watching a ball game and chatting up one of the models, while at a specially set-up table in the lounge Tobey Maguire, Ben Affleck, real estate mogul Bob Safi, Cirque du Soleil creator Guy Laliberté, technology billionaire Alec Gores, World Series of Poker champ Jamie Gold, *The Hangover* director Todd Phillips, *Notebook* director Nick Cassavetes, and myself are playing super high-stakes, no-limit Texas Hold'em poker.

Overseeing things is Molly Bloom, a smart, beautiful, ambitious twenty-seven-year-old who would go on to write about nights like these in her lackluster book *Molly's Game*, later miraculously made into the Academy Award–nominated movie from veteran writer and first-time director Aaron Sorkin. But she didn't tell the whole story. She didn't tell half the story. Hell, she barely even knew the real story.

More on Molly later. Right now, the blinds have been raised to $500/$1,000 and everyone is rolling deep. There are bottles of Dom Pérignon and Cristal open, and when they haven't been attending to the needs of the players, the girls have been in and out of the bathroom to "powder their noses" all night long.

I'm totally focused on the game, however. In my left hand is the only thing I ever drink at the table, a supercold diet raspberry Snapple iced tea. My right hand is covering my cards. If I win this next pot, I'll be up five hundred thousand dollars for the night. Everyone but Jamie and me have folded, and he's just gone all-in: I watch as he pushes every chip he's got into the center of the table.

Todd whistles softly, and one of the girls gives a little gasp— whether in shock or excitement, I don't know. The rest of the room goes quiet. Even Leo turns his attention away from the model who is sitting on his lap and leans forward. I don't take my eyes off Jamie, but next to me I can sense Tobey grinning like a schoolboy.

It is, as they say, a moment. Half a million on the turn of a card. Has life ever felt any better than this?

I call the bet. I had been picking off Jamie's bluffs all night long, but now he was tired of it. He yells: "I've got it this time, Houston!" and turns over two kings. Tobey almost did a spit take.

Yes, Jamie finally had a hand . . . but so did I. I snap called and turned over pocket aces. We ran the entire board three times and I scooped it all, winning nearly $500k for the night.

I gave Tobey a ride home after the game, and I remember him saying with a devilish grin on his face, "If we keep this up we'll eventually take this game for over a billion dollars!" I replied, "Yeah . . . one day they'll call it 'The Billion-Dollar Hollywood Heist.'" We both laughed as my Mercedes CL 65AMG sped down Sunset Blvd.

If you think you know this story because you've read Molly's book, or seen director Aaron Sorkin's movie, think again. This is the real tale behind the richest, most outrageous, and most star-studded high-stakes poker sting in the world.

CHAPTER 1

AN AMERICAN DREAM

My name is Houston Curtis, and for as long as I can remember, I knew I wanted to be a card sharp. That's sharp with *p*. A card shark is someone who is good at playing cards ... but a card sharp, or card mechanic, is someone who can control the outcome of a card game using deceptive methods. And I was a natural. I hustled my first hand of poker aged ten and was bottom dealing, riffle stacking, and performing overhand run-ups before I was fifteen. I could clean out anyone I knew by the age of eighteen, when I left the innocence of the Midwest for Los Angeles to make my fortune in the entertainment business. But I never expected my skills with a deck of playing cards or my love of gambling to take me all the way to a place at Hollywood's most exclusive high-stakes poker game ... or to see me concoct a high-stakes fishing expedition with Tobey Maguire to hook some of the richest and most famous fish in the ocean.

It was a hell of a plan—and a hell of a ride. I saw things and did things most people could only dream about. There were A-list movie stars, private jets, sporting idols, billionaires, gangsters, drink, drugs, Playboy playmates, and thousand-dollar-a-night hookers ... and millions in cash won and lost every week. And when it all came crashing down, I crashed hardest.

Remember that old saying: there are three sides to every story, yours, mine, and the truth? We're going to have to adapt that.

When Molly Bloom published her account of the stellar rise and spectacular fall of our poker ring in 2014, she raised a lot of eyebrows. People were named—I was named, for Christ's sake—and no blushes, it seemed, were spared.

And to coin a phrase I learned from my brother Jimmy back in southern Illinois . . . For the most part, it was all horseshit!

Then Aaron Sorkin turned it into a hit movie, with Jessica Chastain as Molly and journeymen actor Bill Camp playing me (subtly disguised to be twenty years older than I was at the time, going bald, and, for some reason, as "Harlan Eustace"). Michael Cera plays Tobey Maguire, which is pretty funny to anyone who knows either of those guys. And apart from the stand-in for Viper Room owner Darin Feinstein and of course "Bad" Brad Ruderman, the man whose financial tailspin brought the whole thing crashing down and saw us all interviewed by the Feds, Tobey and I were the only two people from the LA game who really mattered to the story Sorkin told.

The movie got a few things right. Molly was certainly beautiful, smart, and driven. But was she the true mastermind behind the most exclusive multimillion-dollar poker game in Tinseltown history? That, as they say in the biz . . . was pure Hollywood, baby.

There are three sides to this story: Molly's version, Sorkin's version, and the truth. And if you think they're the same, keep reading—you are in for a big surprise.

I know what the truth is because I lived it. And if, for the most part, real life is usually nowhere near as exciting as the movies, that is simply not the case in this instance. The real story about the biggest poker game in Hollywood history has far more drama than anything portrayed in Sorkin's screenplay or Molly's book.

Don't get me wrong: it's not their fault. They both simply failed to grasp the one fundamental reason the game existed in the first place.

What if I were to tell you that the whole thing was designed entirely as a hustle from the very beginning? That Tobey and I planned every last detail to give ourselves a huge advantage?

Like the fact that the two of us staked Leonardo DiCaprio to play just so we could attract rich suckers who would dump their money to us?

What if I told you that it wasn't simply a bunch of guys kicking back and enjoying a game of poker every week—albeit for astronomical sums of money—and actually a rigorously planned and meticulously executed business venture?

These things are true, but they are also only the tip of the iceberg.

The biggest game in Hollywood didn't start at The Viper Room. It really started the night I palled up with Tobey Maguire playing high-stakes Hold'em at the Commerce casino in LA in January of 2004. Neither of us had a clue at the time, but that night would end up changing both of our lives forever.

And to understand how that happened, you've got to understand how I came to be in a position to be sharing a table at the Commerce with Hollywood royalty in the first place.

When I rolled into LA as a sharp-eyed and ambitious eighteen-year-old, I didn't know a living soul, other than my two best friends, Steve and Dave, who moved there with me from the cornfields of southern Illinois. We had all played in a rock band together since we were fifteen and figured attending a contemporary music school (The Grove School of Music) would be a great excuse to avoid the agony of a four-year college while living it up in Hollywood. Sure, I wanted to get a record deal and become rich and famous . . . who wouldn't? But I had serious plans for myself whether music panned out for me or not. As it turned out, music led me into the television business.

I was hired for some session work on a TV show called *Showtime at The Apollo,* produced by the legendary variety show producer Bob Banner, who had created such hits as *The Carol Burnett Show, Star Search*, and *Solid Gold.* I would go up to this house in the Hollywood Hills to a recording studio and record sound-alikes for the Pointer Sisters, Bob Marley, and tons of other famous R&B artists who had once played at the Apollo theater in New York. Turns out they didn't want to pay the license fee to use the real music, so I was hired to do "sound-alikes." Hell . . . It was my first gig and already it felt like a hustle. Unfortunately, the 50-dollar session fees I was getting paid weren't gonna pay the bills, so I ended up working for Bob Banner Associates as a full-time production assistant and all-around gopher. With a day job, a band at night, and poker, I was determined to be successful, even if that meant starting at the bottom.

My plan was a radical—and admittedly slightly fucked-up—take on the American Dream. One, I was gonna roll the dice on trying to get a record deal, two, I was going to work damn hard to get as far as I could in the entertainment industry, and three, I was going to deploy a secret skill I had slowly been perfecting since I was a young boy to help me strike it rich. That skill was the ability to manipulate a deck of playing cards as good if not better than anyone in the country. I was a card mechanic, and a good one at that.

For the uninitiated, a card mechanic is someone who knows how to control the outcome of a card game by manipulating the cards in plain sight using false shuffles, false cuts, stacking techniques, and other sleight-of-hand feats that take years to master. Some people might call it cheating . . . but I always preferred to call it "advantage play." Truth be told, I always made an effort to target the suckers who not only deserved to lose, but who could afford to lose. Whenever I had a question of conscience, I was reminded of the immortal words of S. W. Erdnase, the mysterious author of the 1902 classic *The Expert at the Card Table*: "All men who play for any considerable stakes are looking for the best of it," he wrote. Words to live by.

Luckily this was LA, and radical, fucked-up takes on the American Dream is what this town is all about. And also, the two sides to my plan went hand in hand. Scraping together the cash to buy my way into midstakes games, I landed at tables with people in the industry and then used these connections to score gigs as a production assistant and runner—even as I took their money at the poker table. In those days (the 90s), before the Texas Hold'em craze, most of the private games in Hollywood were dealer's choice. This was a perfect scenario for a young, hungry card man to start building a serious bankroll.

While most successful card sharps play with a team or a "mob," in those days I was a lone wolf, which made deploying deception at the card table that much more thrilling, and of course dangerous. Trust me, there's no bigger rush than ringing in a cooler when being offered the cut and handing it back to a guy who is about to deal you the winner and himself the loser in the biggest pot of the night! Having said that, I was careful not to deploy such tactics in most of the entertainment industry games. I needed those guys to like me, to put me up for jobs, recommend me to their industry buddies, and most importantly to invite me back . . . and cleaning them out of all their cash straightaway would not have exactly endeared me to them. A lesson I had learned as a kid watching card players and pool hustlers strategically dismantle the competition at the local southern Illinois bars where my dad spent his days drinking, playing music, and getting the best of it at games of chance.

I'll never forget when a friend of my dad's whom I had never met before showed up at Billy Tom Cody's tavern located in a tough-as-nails little town of Wamac, Illinois. My dad told a couple local guys that he was his cousin Donnie from Tennessee and he loved to gamble at the pool table. I was barely six years old at the time, and I sat and watched my father and his cousin play all day long. On our way home Dad pulled into a factory parking lot about a mile down the road where Donnie was waiting for him in a brand-new red Cadillac. I watched in awe as Donnie took out a giant wad of cash from a bread bag and gave half of it to my dad. Then he turned to me and said, "Lesson #1, kid . . . always keep 'em dancin'!" When I told my dad that I never knew he had a cousin named Donnie from Tennessee, he said, "I don't, boy. That man's real name is Minnesota Fats." It would be a few years later before I fully realized that my dad had hustled the toughest bar in town with one of the top pool sharps in the country as his silent partner. I guess you could say my education started early.

One of the first things I learned back then about hustling games of chance is not just how to win—but how to win just enough to keep the other guy losing. Only win what the other guy can afford to lose and still come back to lose to you again, that's the trick. Where's the profit in taking you for ten thousand tonight and never having you play again, when I can take three thousand off you this time . . . and another three thousand three more times after? The real jackpot lies in finding a whale so big and oblivious that he will keep going into his pocket forever. Music and showbiz aside, that was certainly something I was always keeping an eye out for.

Against all odds, both sides of my plan were working beautifully. Within a few years of starting as a production assistant for Bob Banner, I had a promising career producing syndicated television shows (not bad for a poker-playing musician in his mid-twenties without a college degree), and all of my new entertainment industry contacts were paying off on the side too, as I kept getting invites to bigger poker games.

By the late 90s, I worked my way up to being a development executive at MTV earning six figures a year by day while bringing in another $50k a year by night in poker games. But I still hadn't found my million-dollar idea—the stroke of brilliance that changes the world. In 1999, and in conjunction with a friend I'd known since kindergarten, I found it: coming up with the idea to release a series of videotapes featuring teenage boys beating the hell out of one another and jumping off their parent's roofs onto a bed of thumbtacks and barbed wire. That's right . . . I'm the guy behind the *Best of Backyard Wrestling* video series, a pop-culture hit in the early 2000s that I created with Rick Mahr, my childhood friend from Illinois.

I admit, it wasn't *Driving Miss Daisy*, but it made us both millionaires and I was proud of it nonetheless. For a guy who had never taken a book home all through high school, this was quite a leap.

Life was good. I felt like I was achieving everything I had ever dreamed of. I met and married my beautiful wife, Bonnie Buckley. Talk about a step up. Bonnie and I came from two different worlds: hers being that of a bicoastal debutante who lived with her parents in their Holmby Hills mansion, and mine being that of the card-hustling dreamer from small-town America. Her father threw us a million-dollar wedding with the reception held in the famed Crystal Ballroom of the Beverly Hills Hotel. We were featured in bridal magazines and *Town and Country*. We had doves flying over the crowd as we walked out of the church in Beverly Hills to get in a horse-drawn carriage.

And my poker ambitions? That was coming up roses, too. Soon after getting married, I won a Legends of Poker championship event, besting the 1998 World Series of Poker WSOP champ, Scotty Nguyen, at the final table. In addition to the prize money, I received the coveted Legends of Poker championship ring. They even put my picture up at LA's Bicycle Casino for a year. Then a video game company came along and paid me and my partner another million bucks to turn our Backyard Wrestling videos into a game for Xbox and Sony PlayStation.

I'd done it, right? I'd lived the dream. I'd arrived in LA with nothing but a guitar strapped on my back, a pack of cards in my pocket, and a shitload of ambition. Within a little more than a decade, I'd forged a multimillion-dollar career, met and married the love of my life, and proved I could hold my own straight up against the best poker players in the world. And maybe that should have been enough.

But then, did you ever hear what happened to the boy who got everything he ever dreamed of? He only wanted more, that's what. And Lord knows I was about to get it.

As my bankroll grew, so did my appetite at the card table, and I started finding myself in big games with big names. I was at Hollywood Park the first time Ben Affleck ever decided to play publicly: he showed up with tournament pro Amir Vahedi. My usual pot limit Hold'em game suddenly got swarmed with big guns who were all there in hopes of getting a piece of Ben. It fascinated me to see how excited these guys were to share the table with a movie star.

Affleck was just learning the game at the time, so he was pretty damn ripe in those days. Before long, Ben, Amir, and I had been joined by pros Antonio Esfandiari and Gabe Thaler, as well as WSOP champ Huck Seed—and Ben was getting chopped up all night.

He finally got involved in a huge pot with Gabe, and Ben wanted to raise the stakes in the middle of the hand, which was unprecedented—especially in a licensed casino. It was a pot-limit game, so technically you weren't allowed to raise more than the amount of money that was already in the pot. Affleck turned to Gabe after seeing a seven-high flop and cool as anything says, "Do you wanna just make this hand no limit?"

And what I heard next, I will never forget. Gabe politely asks, "Is that a legitimate offer, sir?"

Affleck says, "Absolutely!"

Gabe called. Affleck showed pocket 10s, Gabe turned over pocket queens and busted Ben for every cent he had on him. It was a great lesson for Ben, one I'm sure he remembers to this day.

Not that it put him off, mind you. I would wind up seeing Ben around quite a bit before our friendly neighborhood Spider-Man ever entered the scene. One week Ben was at the Bicycle Club playing with WSOP gold bracelet winner Annie Duke. He was dating Jennifer Lopez at the time, and J-Lo must have been trying to reach him because all of a sudden someone on the loudspeaker announced: "Ben Affleck, you have a call at the host's desk. Ben Affleck, you have a call from Jennifer at the host's desk!" He was so embarrassed.

Ben also played with me in a Beverly Hills game along with local legend Asher Dan and his cronies. One night in particular, tennis superstar Pete Sampras was in the game as well as LA Laker Rick Fox.

I'll never forget a hand I had with Sampras. He lost a huge pot to me with queens when I flopped a straight. Sampras says: "Damn queens!" then quick as a flash, Rick Fox replies, "Well, Pete, I guess you can only be the best in the world at one sport!"

Everyone started laughing. Then Sampras mentioned the queens again and Affleck interrupted, saying: "Queens? Try living with a fucking queen!" For some reason the joke seemed to escape everyone at the table but me. Perhaps because I remember J-Lo hunting him down in the casino that night. When I cracked a smile, Ben held up a glass to toast me, saying, "You got it, didn't you, Houston?"

He was a funny guy. And a fun guy to play with. Ben would eventually become a solid player as well as a semiregular in our game post-Viper Room, even bringing good buddy Matt Damon along for the ride. Matt was every bit as nice as you'd think he would be. What impressed me most was the fact that when Ben introduced us, Matt had already been given the lowdown by Ben on everyone at the table. He said, "Oh yeah . . . you're the Backyard Wrestling guy Ben was telling me about."

As nice a guy as Matt was, he certainly wasn't the poker player he portrayed on the big screen in *Rounders*. I took him for about fifty grand that night, to which Affleck had to write the check because Matt didn't have enough on him to cover it. We invited him to come back anytime, but truth be told, that was the only time Damon ever played in the big game. He just didn't have the gamble in him like Ben or the rest of us. He wasn't interested.

Now my professional successes with home video franchises like Backyard Wrestling and Ghetto Brawls, as well as the contacts I was making in the Hollywood poker world, were seeing me placed at bigger and bigger games—and private games, not just casino nights. And as a general rule, the bigger the game, the bigger the names involved.

One of the biggest games I had played in at that point was with attorney and Hollywood power broker, Jon Moonves, held at the home of tech millionaire Regan Silber, which got written up in *Vanity Fair* as the "Billionaire Boys Club." I had first met Jon when I was running development for Vin Di Bona's company, the creator of *America's Funniest Home Videos*, because Jon was his attorney and I dealt with his office on all of our deals. Jon shared my love for poker, and we wound up hitting it off while sitting at the same table one time at Hollywood Park. Attorneys tend to get typecast as assholes and crooks, but to this day, I believe Jon Moonves has more class and integrity than 99 percent of the people I've come across both at the poker tables and in show business. I've always been proud to call him a friend. Of course Jon never had a clue that I was a card mechanic and I never put those skills to work in his presence despite being tempted to on many occasions. I had too much respect for the guy. Not to mention, he was overly observant at the table . . . probably because he was used to dealing with the biggest liars and cheaters in Hollywood every day at the office.

We even ended up producing and releasing a series of poker instructional videos together, featuring WSOP Champion Phil Hellmuth and Annie Duke, as well as the television series *The*

Ultimate Blackjack Tour, which aired on his brother's network, CBS.

In addition to being a great guy and amazing dealmaker, Jon was also one hell of a good poker player. Moonves would come to The Viper Room a few times later on, but he was ultimately too conservative (or too smart) to play in the really big games where the swings could knock your lights out.

It was Jon who introduced me to many of the big Hollywood games around town, including Reagan Silber's game. Reagan was a former class-action lawyer from Texas who won a few big cases, then invested in a tech stock that went through the roof, and now he was living in LA exploring options in the entertainment business. He also got me on the invite list to uber-Producer Jon Landau's game, which was lower stakes and more of a "hang" than anything else, but a great place to network with other entertainment industry types and the occasional actor like David Schwimmer, who was a regular. Schwimmer was brutal to play with because he took forever to make a decision over even a small amount of money. Plus, he whined just like his character on *Friends*. He really was Ross . . . only in real life, it's not funny, it's annoying.

Jon also introduced me to Hank Azaria's game. Hank's game was a nice little earner, as the gentlemen card sharps from across the pond like to say—or ripe for the pickens, as we like to say back in the Midwest. Plus, if you got lucky, Hank would bust out some killer impressions to keep everyone laughing while you slowly raked in the big pots . . . I remember liking Hank from the start. He seemed like a really solid guy.

With these guys, I was playing in some of the bigger private games in town and doing well for myself. But much like my entertainment career, success wasn't enough—I wanted The Big One. That's when Spider-Man came into my life.

I first met Tobey Maguire by complete chance. I walked into the Commerce to play some poker one night, and the floorman sat me down at a table right next to him. He had a crazy beard at the time and held an unlit cigar in his hand while he was playing. It was bugging everyone at the table, that cigar. You could almost feel them getting agitated by it, as if they were screaming internally: either light the goddamn thing or put it away!

Not me. I watched and I smiled. Tobey knew what he was doing with that fat Arturo Fuente. He was getting in their heads, and anyone who knows anything about poker knows that getting into your opponents' heads, getting under their skin, is halfway to getting a hold of their bankroll. Interesting, I thought.

Some people might have been intimidated or perhaps starstruck by the idea of sharing a game with Spider-Man. Not me. By this time I was in my early thirties, quite successful, and felt I'd been around a bit.

There I was, seated next to Tobey, watching him do his thing with his cigar and seeing the effect it had on the others at the table—how they were simultaneously starstruck and irritated by him and, as a result, they were just ever-so-slightly distracted.

I was interested in him: not as a movie star, but as a fellow player, and because I figured he might be a good fit for some of the other games I was playing.

Throughout the night, Tobey and I began chatting it up a bit. He was a very likable guy and we immediately hit it off. He was pretty new to poker back then, but you could tell he had the makings of a serious talent: he was soaking up knowledge like a sponge, using what he did know well, and learning from every hand he didn't win. But where the other shlubs at the table were quick to praise his every move, I was a bit more critical of Spidey. I think he liked that.

At one point I reraised him with a semibluff on the turn and got him to lay down a big hand. I didn't show my cards, of course, and I could tell it was eating away at him. He wouldn't stop asking me what I had, even after I'd laughed it off a couple of times. He was relentless about knowing whether or not he had made a good call in folding.

I could tell he was trying to use his movie star charm to get me to spill info, laying that goofy lopsided grin on me, all backslaps and friendly punches on the arm. Of course, at this point Tobey didn't know that I could smell a hustle coming from a mile away, but I decided it might be in my best interest to go ahead and tell him that I bluffed him.

Instead of getting pissed like most poker players do when you bluff them off a hand, Tobey became fascinated by it. He was very inquisitive, and I could tell he had the right qualities to become a real student of the game . . . and potentially a seriously good player.

From that exchange, I think it's safe to say that we hit it off pretty well. Conscious that he was a guy who could make for some interesting future games, and also because I genuinely liked the kid, I eased off the gas a little, being careful not to get involved in any big pots with him, not to do anything that might felt him and put him off ever playing me again. By the end of the night we were even sweating each other's hands when only one of us was in the pot. I won about ten grand that night—and Tobey won, as well. Before he took off, I gave him my number and told him to call me if he ever wanted to play in Reagan's game.

Did I expect to hear from him again? Truthfully: yes, I was convinced of it. Tobey could tell I wasn't just another grinder from the Commerce trying to squeeze out some rent money. I knew that we'd not only hit it off on a personal level, but that he was intrigued by me. The way I'd played that bluff, the other tips I'd given him, the way I'd been the only guy at the table not to fall for the cigar thing or be overawed by his celebrity.

And most of all, I knew that in me he'd seen a chance to use what skills he'd already learned to make proper money. Big money.

They say it takes a hustler to know a hustler, which is probably why Tobey and I felt like we had known each other much better than we did. The hustle is everything, there's always an angle to work, a base to cover, a bluff to call, or a weakness to exploit. For the suckers we eventually recruited into our big games, that weakness was the lure of celebrity, exploiting their pride and vanity at simply sitting alongside the likes of Tobey, Leo DiCaprio, or Ben Affleck . . . cracking jokes with *The Hangover* director Todd Phillips or swapping stories with Rick Salomon, most famous for making a sex tape with Paris Hilton.

For Tobey, that angle was money and nothing else. I saw that immediately. And even before he and I came up with our plan to fleece the big fish of La La Land for millions, I had to work a little hustle on him myself. A sharp player I may have been, a known name around town, a respected figure on the poker circuit, and a regular at games containing celebrities . . . but I was no celebrity myself. And that's a clique you can't crash—you have to be invited.

Even though I hadn't received a call from Tobey yet, when I arrived at Reagan Silber's house the next week to play, there he was . . . sitting at the table with a shit-eating grin, ready to get the cards in the air.

I knew Tobey would make the perfect partner to build a game around. At this time he was breaking box-office records as a huge star, so people would dump money just to sit with him, and he was smart enough and rich enough to sustain the game in the long term. So, that night I did something I rarely do. I decided to have a few drinks and allow my game to go ever-so-slightly off the rails. I was playing long ball with Spider-Man and betting it would pay off.

Before the end of the night I had dumped a nice chunk of dough to the game, some of it going to Tobey. Up to this point he had only seen me win, so it was crucial that I prove to him I could be "good for the game."

It was the first step on what was to be a wild ride toward piles of cash, and I was ready for it. I was beating these games every week straight up, which felt weird for me, but in a good way. All the work I'd done since arriving in LA, all the connections I'd made, all the hustles I'd worked up until now was about to pay off in spades . . . This was officially the big leagues.

CHAPTER 2

GAME ON

After Tobey's first game at Reagan's place, the two of us became regulars there for a while, but it quickly became obvious that it simply wasn't the right place, or the right vibe, for what we had in mind. The simple fact that we were living in a celebrity-obsessed town with more than its fair share of suckers carrying more money than sense, the potential to clean up was huge. Don't get me wrong: Silber was a good guy and a great host. He was unfailingly generous and accommodating, and his table always had enough action to ensure a steady source of income for any player who knew what he was doing. But by then it was no longer enough: we had bigger ambitions. Tobey was developing into a genuinely talented player, and very quickly we saw in each other the potential to work together to make serious money.

If we were going to do this properly, we had to have our own game. We had to set the whole thing up on our terms, call our own shots, stack the odds as heavily as we could in our favor . . . and, of course, have as much fun and make as much dough as we could along the way.

But first of all we needed to see if the idea would fly. Tobey and I had an unspoken understanding from that first game. My plan to dump some money had worked like a charm: Tobey not only had fun, he also invited me to a game he was having at his house.

The funny thing is, I think he kinda knew what I was up to . . . and he just dug my vibe. So when Tobey invited me over to his place, it was partly to work out if there was mileage in our own game, and partly to check how well the two of us could work together.

It played out like a dream. That first night he and I riffed off each other beautifully, instinctively, careful again not to fall into reckless all-in, head-to-head confrontations with each other, but also gambling with enough competitiveness that nobody would suspect we were working as any kind of team.

Of course, we didn't have any such qualms about taking down the other guys at the table. They were a mix of industry people, loose buddies of Tobey's, and moneyed-up friends-of-friends; and by the end of the night every single one of them was down several grand. Not bad for a few hours' work.

From then on, we politely backed off from Reagan's game. Tobey set up a regular night at the Maguire Mansion, and the action there soon took on a life of its own.

Tobey lived in a swanky modern house set high in the Hollywood Hills, far along the winding streets that led up from the Sunset Strip. His was a very exclusive neighborhood known as the "bird streets" due to the fact that all of the streets had names like Oriole Drive, Blue Jay Way, and Skylark Avenue. His neighbors included tons of other A-listers and power players, ranging from Christina Aguilera to Rupert Murdoch—and of course his best buddy, Leonardo DiCaprio.

Each house you passed made you wonder not only which famous Hollywood star or power player lived there now, but about all the big names of the past who had called this hillside their home. It also made you wonder exactly what kinds of scandals and secret deeds had happened behind those walls . . . or was still happening now.

Aside from looking cooler than hell and sitting on the side of a hill with an infinity pool that made it look like you could swim out into the sky, Tobey's place was nothing incredibly special— not by the standards of those streets. He had bought it a couple of years before I met him on the tip of a hot real estate broker. It paid off, because he eventually sold it to a young Walton couple, heirs to the Walmart fortune, for around 15 million.

Once a week I'd roll up the beautiful bird streets of West Hollywood, make my way through the grounds to his villa. When I think of that place now, it's always sunset in my mind: perhaps because I usually arrived in the evenings, perhaps because it had one of the most beautiful views of the setting sun in all West Hollywood. I'd often pause for a moment before I entered the house, just to watch the sun dip, boiling orange and violet, over the dreamy Hollywood Skyline . . . always with a tingling sensation in my bones before a big game and the prospect of a major payday.

I'd also take a moment to check out the other cars pulled up in his driveway. In those early days Tobey didn't always fill me in on the guest list beforehand—but a quick scan of the vehicles they drove usually gave a fair idea of what kind of action I might be in for. Tip to the wise: Mercedes drivers generally knew what they were about . . . whereas those who owned Porsches, Ferraris, Lamborghinis, and the like were easy pickings. Too flash, too obvious, too anxious to impress.

Best of all were the guys with their own drivers—especially the ones who insisted their chauffeurs wear full uniform and little peaked cap. The reason? My view's simple: no real gambler ever wanted anyone else to drive him. If you can't or don't want to take control of your own ride, you're just not made for the poker table.

Of course, some of them used drivers because they were planning on drinking heavily. In which case they were doubly fucked before they even began.

Those early games at Tobey's were a lot of fun—but they were nothing compared to what was to follow. The money was definitely getting toward the kinds of places Tobey and I were shooting for, but there was none of the other craziness that would later surround the game. Call girls? Cocaine? Limitless champagne, shoulder rubs by LA's most beautiful models and a hostess on standby to bring whatever you fancied between hands? Not in Tobey Maguire's house!

We played in his fucking kitchen—don't get me wrong, it's a hell of a kitchen, I've known whole apartments smaller than that kitchen—but it was still a kitchen. And not exactly a location scout's first choice of setting for a sordid tale of money, excess, and busted lives, right?

So why did we play in Tobey's kitchen? Simple: that's where he kept his poker table. It was an old-fashioned round table that he had set in a nook in place of a traditional kitchen table. It was funny at first, but after a while it really wasn't working and I was forever riding him to set up the game in the living room in order to class up the atmosphere.

He finally relented the night Jeff Katzenberg dropped over $40k to me. Katzenberg was so bummed out from sitting in that small nook, losing his ass and watching Tobey's private chef make a bunch of horrific vegan treats, that he never returned. It was actually a valuable lesson, in retrospect: if you're planning on mugging someone for their hard-earned cash, at least make them feel like it's being done in the right surroundings. Let them have something positive to take away from the experience.

Having to play in the kitchen wasn't the only one of those early games' peculiarities. Tobey's got a lot of what you might call eccentricities.

He's paranoid about germs, for a start, even to the extent that we all had to take our shoes off when we came in the house and slip on a pair of Crocs. It was kind of weird, especially when a guy like Katzenberg showed up. He's the man responsible for the Lion King, for Christ's sake. He produced Shrek . . . and here's Tobey, who was raised on those films, getting all uptight about whether the billionaire former chairman of Walt Disney Studios has wiped his goddamn shoes on the doormat properly.

Tobey was also sober since before he could drink legally, and although he didn't mind other guys drinking, it's kind of difficult to really cut loose on the booze when you're under the roof of a guy who doesn't touch a drop. It didn't bother me—I like to keep a clear head at the table anyway—but I could see that for some of the others, the idea of a boys' card night without some kind of alcohol-induced raucousness didn't exactly sit right.

The same goes for his veganism. He wasn't about to stop us ordering pepperoni pizza, but he certainly wasn't happy about it. He'd sit there making that face that ex-smokers make when other people light up around them, while on the other side of the room his chef tried to tempt us with weird spinach and quinoa things. We laughed at the time, but Tobey wasn't smiling. It bummed him out just having meat in the house.

In fact, one of the reasons we ended up moving the game from Tobey's house to The Viper Room was that Tobey was, and I quote, "Sick of all these scumbag poker players coming into my house."

And, to be fair, he kind of had a point. Aside from the shoe paranoia, the dead flesh and dairy consumed, and the lingering aroma of beer, champagne, and Jack Daniels in the air, some of the regulars had other peccadilloes that wound Tobey up tight.

I'll never forget the first time I met the one-and-only Kevin Washington, who happened to be the heir to his Montana father's six-billion-dollar fortune and had made a bunch of headlines in places like *Forbes* for having the biggest superyacht in Marina del Rey. Kevin may not have been most people's definition of a scumbag, but he chewed tobacco and spit in one of Tobey's cups, which, while funny as hell to everyone else, made Tobey want to puke in his own mouth.

But despite all that, the bottom line remained the same. "Poker scumbags" they may have been, but in just a few months Tobey and I chopped up more money in that kitchen than his private chef did with a year's supply of lettuce. There were so many dollars flowing through the game that we had to invest in a professional cash machine to check all the rebuys and payoffs.

It was a whole new level of thrill to me. I still get shivers thinking about sitting in that kitchen watching Jeff Katzenberg write me that forty-eight-thousand-dollar check. Forty-eight grand from Mr. Dreamworks to the guy who produced *Backyard Wrestling* . . . what a rush.

I was playing—and beating—a whole different class of people. And if I was learning just one lesson, it was a very simple one: all the money in the world can't buy you skills at the poker table. And rich, famous, powerful dudes can get taken just as badly and just as brutally as any other sucker.

I recall one night Tobey had invited famed record mogul Guy Oseary round to play: he's the kid who started the Maverick Label for Madonna as a seventeen-year-old and would later go on to be manager of U2 and Amy Schumer. But as good as Oseary was at selling records, his poker skills were far less polished.

I'll never forget at a certain point that evening watching him look down at his hand, nearly jump out of his seat, and yell with nervous excitement, "I'm all-in!"

It was so obvious he had pocket aces that I almost folded my hand without even looking at my cards. Then I gave them a peek and was staring at two kings! What shitty luck. Kings were the only hand other than Aces that I simply refuse to lay down pre-flop if I'm playing the game straight up.

I said to the table: "Guy, you're not only lucky enough to get all your money in with aces, but you're about to get called by the one hand I just can't lay down preflop."

I called and showed the kings . . . and of course, he whooped and turned over two red aces. But this is where Guy's luck ran out. A king came on the flop, and I busted him for everything he had in front of him. What a great feeling!

These may have been the days before the models and Playboy bunnies, but it wasn't just boys at Tobey's place. He had not long met girlfriend Jen Meyer (they eventually tied the knot in 2007, ironically at the height of our hustle, before splitting again in 2017), and he was so loved up he insisted on having her deal. In fact, that's where the idea of tipping instead of raking (taking a percentage of) the pot was born. Tobey would jokingly warn everyone, "If you wanna be invited back, make sure to tip Jen!"

One time I asked him why he didn't just hire a dealer so Jen could play: it was obvious to everyone that she wanted to join in properly. He told me that he didn't like her gambling. Make of that what you will.

That was also when he filled me in on the fact that Jen's dad (who just happens to be Ron Meyer, former president of Universal and amongst the grandest fromages on the whole Hollywood cheeseboard) was a HUGE gambler who had been known to play very high stakes. I asked Tobey if he was any good at poker, and he just gave me that slow, crooked smile. "Let's just say Ron plays with a lot of heart," he said. Which, in hustler code meant that he was dead money. Interesting.

Not long after that night Tobey got a call in the middle of our game, and who should it be . . . but the future father-in-law. He gets off the phone, pulls me aside, and whispers: "Ron Meyer is playing in a game at Gabe Kaplan's house. It's 200/400 pot limit and they've got two seats open!"

We were in the middle of our usual game and the table was full. Strictly speaking, splitting to play somewhere else would pretty much be the height of bad etiquette—but then Tobey shrugged and said: "Jen can keep dealing, let's go chop these guys up!"

I thought, fuck it! Let's do it.

Gabe Kaplan lived nearby, just off Coldwater Canyon, so Tobey and I bailed on our own game and shot down Mulholland to Coldwater as fast as we could. Walking into Gabe's house was like being transported back to the fucking 70s. From the wood panels to the shag carpeting, hell, even the smell of the place was old. You could tell he bought this house in the "Welcome Back Kotter" days and had just been living off of past royalties and fading glory ever since.

I'd never played Gabe, but I knew his reputation—and not just as an old comedian from when I was a kid. He was also a true card hustler. Rumor was Meyer had staked him for several years, and that's basically how Gabe made his living aside from the occasional hosting gig for the *World Series of Poker* on ESPN.

I was interested to see how good he really was, and I knew Ron was the true target of the game, but I couldn't help myself. Despite myself, I ended up getting all-in after the flop with Gabe right out of the gate. I had ace king, he had ace queen, and the flop came ace, king, nine. He stuck all of his money in with the worst of it but hit a miracle suck out as the turn showed a ten and the river a jack, giving him a straight. Seemed almost too good to be true . . . kinda like some of the games I had played in with the LA Russian and Armenian guys who were mobbed up and always trying to line up a double duke. I made a note to keep my eyes on the dealer from that point forward.

It's safe to say that Gabe and I were never going to become pals. I think he saw me as competition. He had been beating all of these Hollywood games for years and figured Tobey and his buddy were just going to be another target. But he learned quickly that wasn't the case. And even though he cracked me for $20k that night, I knew one thing for sure . . . assuming the hand was dealt straight up, he had to get very lucky to beat me. Either way, I knew where I stood with him.

Needless to say, Tobey had a great time taking his new daddy-in-law's dollars and ended up winning huge that night. So huge that it helped solidify the decision to move the game out of his kitchen for good.

By then we were playing at Tobey's at least twice a week and raking in money almost faster than we could count it. I used to wonder sometimes why Tobey allowed me to keep coming, given the amount I was taking out of the game. Eventually a mutual friend of ours, Andy Bellin, who wrote the book *Poker Nation*, told me that Tobey enjoyed playing with me just because he liked the complexity of my game. Simple as that. I was right in the inner sanctum of the hottest game in Hollywood . . . because Spider-Man dug my style.

Of course, amongst all the fun there were sobering moments, too—and, as it turned out, not everyone could afford to be so free with their money as the likes of Katzenberg, Kevin Washington, and Guy Oseary.

There was one instance that really stayed with me for a long time. A guy showed up who was a vice president at Fred Segal in Beverly Hills, which is one of the must-go places for celebs to buy their clothes, which I assume is how Tobey must have known him.

I never asked about the people he invited to the game back then, I was just happy to get a seat. But it became obvious pretty quick why Tobey had invited this cat. The poor bastard lost around $10k the first time he played. The following week he dumped thirty grand to me alone.

I talked to Tobey after the game that night, and he asked me how much a VP of a retail clothing store made a year. I remember laughing and asking him if he was growing a conscience over us busting this poor sap. And the thing is, I actually think he was. Tobey loved winning, but he didn't want to hurt people.

Or, to be more accurate, he didn't want to hurt people who couldn't afford to take the hit.

Anyway, that same dude came back to the game the next week, and I took him for exactly another thirty thousand. The poor guy was almost crying when he got up from the table that night. He couldn't even bring himself to leave. Instead he just sat in the kitchen next to Spidey's private vegan chef and watched the action continue with a glazed-over, wide-eyed stare on his face.

Tobey told me that night he felt the kid was out of his depth and that we shouldn't invite him back. Two weeks later, I found out something that shook me to my core. After not getting invited back, the poor guy committed suicide.

When Tobey told me about it, my heart literally sank into my chest. Apparently Fred Segal VPs didn't make that much dough after all. Between Tobey luring him to the game and me cleaning him out completely, we had effectively destroyed this guy's life. Looking back with the benefit of 20/20 hindsight, that whole incident should have served as a warning for what was to follow with Bad Brad Ruderman.

Perhaps sadly, the guilt didn't last too long. Poker is by definition cruel, and the best players only get to the top by being utterly ruthless with their opponents. Destroying them, cleaning them out . . . it's rough, but it's also kind of the point of the enterprise.

We moved on. And it was time for the game to move on, too.

We were about to really start fleecing some people, and Tobey is nothing if not smart. There's an old British saying: don't shit on your own doorstep—we both knew that inviting someone into your home and basically mugging the poor fucker for all of his dough probably wasn't a sustainable, or very wise, plan in the long term. We needed a venue that combined anonymity with glamour, a place that would serve as a draw in and of itself . . . but at the same time free Tobey from any worries that he wouldn't be directly associated with the fact that people were going broke every week in the game. Very funny in hindsight considering how things ended up.

Also, I didn't say anything out loud, but I couldn't help thinking that relaxing the whole no-shoes, easy-on-the-beer-and-pepperoni policy might help, too.

One day Tobey said, "What about The Viper Room?"

I knew it was perfect straightaway: at once seedy and glamorous enough to sit pretty with both A-list celebs and the millionaire hangers-on we wanted to attract. Johnny Depp was a former owner; River Phoenix had overdosed there . . . and now our mutual buddy Darin Feinstein was in charge of the place.

If you've read Molly's book, Darin is called Reardon; in the film his name is changed again, to Dean. And if she paints him as this hotshot property hustler with questionable morals and a filthy mouth . . . What she failed to mention is that he was a riot to hang out with. Darin could always be kind of a loose cannon, but overall a really fun guy to hang out with. And on top of that, he was superenthusiastic about the idea from the start.

Tobey asked me to call him and asked about having a regular game there. Darin had not long taken over The Viper and he was naturally excited about making it a hot celeb hangout again, so of course he jumped at the chance. What's more, he told me to tell everyone that he would have a "Hot little piece of ass named Molly serve drinks." He said it . . . not me.

It was perfect. By having the game at The Viper Room, it didn't have to "officially" be attached to Tobey at all: everyone would assume he—and I—were just players in the game, like them. And by letting a third party (which ended up being Darin's "hot little piece of ass" named Molly Bloom) assume control of organizing the players and taking care of collecting and paying out the wins and losses, we not only freed ourselves of all the tedious admin crap, but could blend into the background still farther—all the better to work the hustle even harder!

Like I said: a hustler's always hustling. Always looking for a new plan to increase the take. Molly was to be that new plan. As it happens, and for the record, I liked her: I thought of Molly like a little sister, and Tobey was fond of her, too. But make no mistake, whatever else we let her believe, it was Tobey and I who truly ran the game, not Molly.

While Molly is very smart in real life, she is not exactly the righteous character Jessica Chastain portrayed her to be in the film. But smart: yes! Smart enough, in fact, that by the time Darin threatened to pull the game from her, she was already romantically involved with one of the players . . .

But we're getting ahead of ourselves. The real hustle was just beginning. Tobey's Spidey-senses were tingling, and it was time to take it to the next level. Darin and Molly got to work, and we soon got the first of what were to be regular texts from our new hostess, inviting us to The Viper to play.

The game, as Sherlock Holmes used to say, was afoot!

CHAPTER 3

SNAKES IN THE VIPER ROOM

From outside, The Viper Room doesn't look like much: a squat, black, windowless rectangle on the Sunset Strip, wedged between a place selling cigars and a run-down liquor store.

The main entrance is around the side of the building. It was always roped off, and of course, unless you were someone important, you had to wait in a line with all the other hopefuls and hangers-on to get in. After that there's a dark corridor that ended at a small ticket counter where there was usually an attractive girl waiting with a hand stamper. You're then forced to turn right and walk up the stairs in order to get into the club.

Not that we ever had to bother with any of that, of course. No waiting in lines for us, our days of queues and hand stampers were long gone. To get to our game, the pretty girl with the ink stamp would wave us past the ticket counter and through a hidden door in the back.

Once inside our private room, there was a bar along the back of the wall, lounge-style couches covering two of the walls in an L shape and in the center of the room just enough space for a full-size poker table.

It couldn't have been more of a contrast to Tobey's spotlessly antiseptic kitchen: it was dark, dingy, and smelled permanently of piss and stale beer . . . and for all those reasons I loved it. This blacked-out basement with LA's hottest up-and-coming bands literally above our heads held a filthy, seductive charm that we knew would pull in just the right kind of people.

This was a place to really play poker. This was a place to start winning big.

Tobey and I had plenty of discussions leading up to our first night at The Viper. We'd mapped out a sure-fire three-step strategy to ensure the games success. If we were going to do this at all, we were going to do it properly. Step one, have a shill fronting the game to take any unnecessary heat off of Tobey or any of the "regulars" for that matter. Step two, invite players with more money than sense, and step three, stock the pond with big celebs so the little fishies would keep swimming back week after week!

Step one of our strategy had already been set in place by Darin. We needed someone to make the phone calls every week and set up the game, get refreshments, keep track of the buy-ins, and make sure everyone settled up at the end of the night. Best of all, once Darin suggested Molly we knew we wouldn't even have to pay her anything to do it: we'd just recycle Tobey's "tip the hostess if you want to come again" trick. She'd make a bunch of easy money, and we'd stay under the radar and avoid all the administration crap. Sweet!

Of course, we only seriously expected her to make a few hundred bucks at a time: it's a testament to both her ambition and the sheer size and scale of the game we created that she regularly took home tens of thousands in tips at the end of the night.

Also, to be fair to her, however it ended, Molly was perfect at the start. And now that we had a proper venue and her face to hide behind, it was time for us to cut loose.

Make no mistake. We weren't running this game for the love of poker. This was no gentlemanly battle of wits, no social get-together between friends. We were there to win money, pure and simple. Hell, it wasn't even a fair fight. The odds were stacked in our favor from the start. That was the whole point of it.

Right out of the gate, the entire game was designed to empty the pockets of the uninitiated, the celeb-loving, rich LA suckers. Millionaire trust-fund types and heirs to offshore fortunes. Guys who'd made a killing on Wall Street, or in tech start-ups, or on the Internet, or by lucking out on the back of someone else's talent: in short, men with more money than they knew what to do with. Men who weren't necessarily very good at poker—but who wouldn't mind writing a six-figure check every now and then for the thrill of getting to sit next to some genuine Hollywood big shots.

Molly was theoretically organizing it, of course, but we knew what kind of action we wanted to attract, so we put a plan together in order to achieve our goal, which meant bypassing Darin and dealing with Molly directly. Hell, Darin didn't want the responsibility anyway. I was texting and talking with Molly so damn much in those first weeks, I had to explain who the hell she was to my wife, Bonnie, with the assurance that everything was "strictly business."

The most important thing for Tobey was to kick things off with a boom. He wanted his longtime buddy Leonardo DiCaprio to be a part of the game right out of the gate. As big of a star as Tobey was at the time, there was arguably no celebrity in all Hollywood bigger than Leo. We knew that if we could spread the word around town there was a private poker game at The Viper Room with huge celebs like Tobey and Leo playing, it wouldn't take long before our bait attracted some huge fish.

It's the oldest trick in the networker's book: connections. Sure, Tobey was a draw himself, but if playing poker and shooting the breeze with Spider-Man was one kind of thrill, how much more thrilling to be doing it with Tobey Maguire and Leonardo DiCaprio? And, say, Ben Affleck? Alongside the guy who made millions out of banging Paris Hilton and videotaping it? In the basement of the place where River Phoenix got himself fatally fucked up on coke and heroin speedballs?

That first game was to be on a Tuesday, so Tobey and I got together over the weekend to go over the lineup. That's when Tobey told me that in order to get Leo to play we were going to have to stake him.

I actually laughed in his face. "Stake DiCaprio? What the fuck?"

Why in all hell would a guy like Leo need to be staked? The kid was as rich as Croesus for crying out loud. He could afford to wipe his ass with hundred-dollar bills—in what crazy world would he need funding by us?

Tobey laughed right back. "Because he's no idiot," he said. "And he knows exactly why we want him to be there."

If Leonardo DiCaprio was going to be the juicy bait wriggling on our hook that would attract the fattest fish in Tinseltown, then it stood to reason he wasn't going to put up his own money to do it. The way he saw it, he was doing us a favor by being there at all, and if we wanted him to play, we could damn well cover the cost of it.

I guess I could understand that. I mean—he was doing us a favor, and in all fairness, we did only want him there for his pulling power. God knows we didn't want him there for his action—he was tighter than a gnat's ass. But still: it never ceases to amaze me how these celebs are always getting free rolled through life!

I remember being at Leo's house one day after the game had been running for a while. Tobey was supposed to meet me there.

While I was waiting, Leo offered to give me the grand tour. The place was incredible, obviously, but the thing that really stuck in my memory was when he told me how Giorgio Armani had agreed to make custom covers for every piece of furniture in the house. And believe me: it's a big house, there's a whole lot of furniture.

And like a kid who just got away with robbing the candy store, Leo grinned and gave me the kicker: " . . . and all I gotta do for it," he said, "is wear an Armani suit to three red carpet events! And I usually wear Armani anyway!"

The point being, once you have enough fame and money to buy anything you want, apparently everything becomes free. Talk about a hustle . . . sign me up.

And so it was again: here was Leo, one of the wealthiest celebs in the business and a guy who loves a hand or two of Hold'em . . . but in order to get him to sit at the table, Tobey and I were putting up the money for him to play. And of course there was no point in asking Tobey why he wouldn't just cover him on his own (being another multimillionaire Hollywood star and all) . . . because I knew what the answer was already. Tobey was more than aware that I was going to be getting just as much out of having Leo there as he was—and that meant splitting the cost.

So . . . Leo was in, but only on a free roll from me and Tobey. That meant that if he lost, we would have to cover his losses, but if he won, we would keep fifty percent of his wins.

The good news was that Leo was actually a pretty conservative player—what seasoned guys would call a "nut-peddling squeezer," who only got involved in hands where he held aces and kings. It meant he was unlikely to win spectacularly—but it also meant he minimized his losses. Bottom line, when you combine the fat fish

Leo would draw to the game with the fact that the buy-in we staked him with might as well have been the life savings of a commerce grinder looking to make his rent money . . . we weren't actually too worried about losing a penny with Mr. DiCaprio. That being said, the principle of it still kind of irked me.

After getting Leo locked in, the next thing we needed—besides a room full of suckers—was going to be a professional dealer who could bring a proper table and professional poker chips, so we wouldn't have to sweat anyone trying to smuggle their own chips into the game.

There was only one guy I trusted with this job. His name was Manny Lopez. Manny had been dealing to me for years at the Hollywood Park Casino and in tons of other private games around town. What I knew about Manny was this . . . he was a hardworking, honest guy who rarely gambled himself and didn't even care to play poker. He learned how to deal as a way of supporting his family, and every month he would send money back to many of them who still lived in Mexico.

But most of all, I knew Manny wasn't a card mechanic: there would be no manipulation of the deck under Manny's watch, as he was as straight as they come. How did I know this? Because when you've been able to control the outcome of a poker game with a deck of cards as long as I have, the one thing you know how to spot is someone else who does the same. And Manny dealt as straight as a Baptist preacher.

In Molly's book she calls Manny "Diego"—nice racial stereotyping there, Molly!—and passes him off as if he were nothing more than a bit of hired help. In fact, Manny played just as big a role as Molly did to our game. He got tipped the same amount as her, and most crucially, what Molly didn't know is that Manny would often give me full reports on everything that would go down with Molly at the end of each night.

So we had the venue, the hostess, the A-list bait, and a professional dealer. The next thing to do was increase the action, and that meant raising the blinds.

For the uninitiated, a blind bet is a forced bet that goes around the table just in front of the button, which represents the dealer. There is a small blind and a big blind. Since we were having a professional center dealer (like you see in today's tournament poker on ESPN), the button is required so players know when it is their turn to act. It's basically a way of kicking off the betting: you've got to match the big blind if you want to be in the pot.

When we were playing at Tobey's house the blinds started out at $10/20 then quickly got raised to $20/40 and then to $50/100. Say you've got nine guys around the table and they all limp in to see the flop—well there's nearly a thousand dollars in the pot before anyone's even thought about raising a real bet.

Of course every time the blinds got raised, the game played bigger. We were now going to make the blinds $100/200, meaning the minimum amount of money anyone could get into the pot for would be 200 dollars. And the maximum? No limit, baby.

And then we pulled off something really smart. The blinds were $100/200, but we deliberately set the buy-in to be as small as we could credibly get away with. Five grand ought to do it, we figured.

Believe it or not, this was almost as crucial to our initial plan as getting players like Leo involved. Admittedly, to those without a nose for a hustle it sounds kind of crazy. If the whole idea is to take as much money as possible out of these suckers, then surely, you'd think, you want to set the buy-ins good and high, right?

Have them dump a shitload of dollars down from the get-go and then siphon it all off through the night?

That's what you'd think. But Tobey and I were smarter than that.

All this was happening around 2005, so poker was still taking off in mainstream popularity and gaining interest from new players all the time. And a lot of these newcomers didn't really understand "poker structure" back then—so when they heard that it was just a measly five thousand to buy in, they were psyched. Five grand to play at the Viper with big shot celebrities—hell, that wasn't just cheap, that was the sale of the century!

But in reality, with the blinds set at $100/200, five thousand dollars is a pitifully tiny amount of money to have in front of you. By comparison, if you were to play a cash game in a casino with the blinds set at that level, most guys would have around $50k in front of them, just to cover any blips along the way.

Anyone who knows poker knows that five grand was only going to last you a few bets with blinds this high.

Of course, five thousand was the minimum buy-in, but by no means the maximum. And it goes without saying that so long as you were good for the money, you could keep reloading with another five gees as many times as you liked.

Here's how it panned out, every single time. Tobey and I would sit down with ten or twenty grand to start so we had everybody at the table covered. And like clockwork, every time the button had made it all the way around everyone once, at least two players would have gone completely broke and had to reload.

It was a hustle so basic, so obvious, as to almost be laughable. But it worked. The players we were recruiting didn't have a clue about any of that. These guys would be out of chips from their first buy-in after two hands and then what do they do? Walk away from the most star-studded night of their lives ten minutes after arriving? Hell no! They would always man up and reload, and five grand became ten. And then fifteen, twenty, twenty-five . . . and they would keep reloading until they had to call Daddy for another advance from the trust fund.

It was beautiful to see, like an old-school kind of "bait and switch" scam. You show up to the car dealership because the ad said you could get a great used car for five thousand bucks . . . but once you're there you end up spending fifty grand for the same damn car just because you've been bamboozled by a good sales-man! Well, in this scenario Tobey and I were the salesmen and we were selling the idea of hanging out with celebs in an exclusive environment with the chance of winning money, while only having to risk a few thousand.

In reality most of the guys who attended the game never had a chance of winning. Let's be honest: that's why they were there in the first place. And nobody's ever going to get up and leave once their first five grand's gone: not from that company: they'd feel embarrassed and stupid. Of course they're gonna rebuy!

It was not unusual for geeks who'd arrived swearing they were only going to spend five, maybe ten thousand maximum to end up writing checks for sums well over $100,000.

But here's the thing: the longer they stayed, and the more money they dumped, the more they could convince themselves it was worth it. That they were a part of something special. That's what they were paying for.

The final step of our plan was for Manny in the dealer's chair to use a professional Shuffle Master machine to shuffle the cards. Normally, this would go against everything I believe in when it comes to a card hustle. But Tobey had no idea I was a professional card mechanic. Hell, no one did—and I wasn't about to start shouting about it now. It was and has been the single biggest secret I've ever kept in my life until now.

Also, I knew I would still be able to use my card mechanics throughout the course of a night. There'd always be a little side action going on, and so, for example, if anyone ever wanted to gamble with me to see who could cut to the highest card, it was child's play for me to make sure I was a guaranteed winner every time. (Literally child's play—that's a trick I've been doing since I was an actual child.)

One time I won fifty thousand on the single turn of a card against a guy who was half in the bag and looking for a way to lose money. Fifty grand for pulling off a hustle I used to practice at elementary school!

And every now and then when Manny would take a break, I would jump in the dealer's seat and subtly forgo the Shuffle Master altogether. Nobody ever suspected that with two or three shuffles I could deal any hand I wanted. I remember serving Leo pocket aces once when I sat in for Manny. Since I had 50 percent of his action, I figured, why the hell not?

All that aside, the point about having Manny and a Shuffle Master working full-time was that we were able to get off as many hands as possible per hour. The more hands we could get dealt, the more money we could make, simple as that. At first we used a professional Shuffle Master Tobey bought and he would charge the game 200 bucks every time we used it, which both of us laughed about on many occasions. Later, the game just chipped in and bought our own. It wasn't cheap, either! Back then, you had to know someone in the casino industry to even get your hands on one of these things, and once you did it would cost you around fifteen grand!

But you know what they say . . . time is money! And the Shuffle Master was quite literally a time-saving, hand-spitting money maker.

CHAPTER 4

HOOKING THE FISH

Even now, over a decade later, I still look back on that first game as one of the defining moments of my life. Not only did it go exactly to plan, but it set in motion a chain of events and introduced a roll call of people who would eventually change things for me forever. For good . . . and for bad.

That first night Tobey and Leo had followed me down the Sunset Strip to The Viper Room, and when we arrived, movie director Todd Phillips was already there, leaning up against the wall outside having a smoke and looking like a typical LA hood rat. I had met Todd before, playing Pot Limit Hold'em at Hollywood Park with his agent, and he had to be one of the funniest guys I knew. Everything Todd said made people crack up.

But he's also a natural born gambler. I remember one night we were playing and he said, "Man, I'm pretty excited about the deal I just carved out with this new film I directed." Todd rarely talked about work, so I was interested to hear what he had to say.

He explained he had taken a punt on the film by giving up his director's fee of seven or eight million bucks in order to score a healthy chunk of the back end—essentially betting his entire wage on the movie's success. Well, guess what. That movie was *The Hangover*, and his gamble would ultimately make him worth over a hundred million dollars. Boom!

The four of us hadn't gotten halfway down the corridor into the club when I heard the boisterous voice of former Callaway Golf CEO Bruce Parker. Bruce was loud and a bit of an annoying bastard, but in a good way. Good for the game at least.

When we entered our dark, seedy little room, we saw Bruce was chatting up a beautiful young girl . . . who turned out to be the infamous Miss Molly Bloom. Molly was very polite and professional out of the gate, despite her obvious nerves, but she is prone to a little exaggeration now and then. Contrary to what her book might have you believe, for example, nobody handed Molly cash to buy in. It was a "gentlemen's game." Everyone started out with $5k in chips, and if someone wanted more, they would sign for them. And we always settled up at the end of the night, no questions asked.

Next to enter was Dean Factor—and that's "Factor" as in heir to the Max Factor fortune. I had already played with Dean a few times. One time was at the Playboy Mansion, where I ended up at the final table of a charity poker event with Don Cheadle. I pushed all-in with pocket kings and Cheadle called with queen, jack preflop for his entire stack and ended up getting a straight. Bastard. But hey, it was for charity, so who cares, right?

For some reason, when I first met him, Dean kinda rubbed me the wrong way. I never really had a problem fitting in with rich dudes and high rollers so long as they were self-made or at least refused to live off the back of their rich families. But Dean just kinda came off as a rich dickhead. His demeanor was that of someone who felt entitled to win . . . which just made me want to make him my bitch. And, of course, that is exactly what I was planning to do that first night at The Viper Room.

So with Bruce Parker, Dean Factor, Todd Phillips, Tobey, and Leo, we were only missing a few more players. In walked Steve

Brill. Brill was also a comedy film director. He was the guy who had done all those Mighty Ducks movies. Rumor was, he sued Disney over the use of the Mighty Ducks name and ended up getting blackballed in the industry. By the time I met him, he was the guy Adam Sandler would use to direct a lot of his films including *Mr. Deeds* and *Little Nicky.*

The first time I ever won over $20k in a pot had been from Brill when I busted him in Tobey's kitchen. Like Todd, he was a funny guy, but Brill had more of a temper and would whine like a little girl when he lost. He was also about the only poker player I knew who could manage to get under Tobey's skin. There was something about him that would set Tobey off almost every time we played.

It was always funny watching Tobey get steamed at Brill. It was usually because Brill was questioning a call or taking forever to make a decision on a hand. To Tobey's credit, Brill could really come off as an asshole when he wanted to. Even still, I always liked the guy. He's the kind of guy who could make you laugh even when he was directly insulting you. One time he made a comment about my hair after I felted him, claiming it looked like I had a Lhasa Apso on my head.

After Brill in walked my buddy Andy Bellin. Andy had recently written a book called *Poker Nation* and was used to the private underground games of New York. Jon Moonves and I had used Andy as a consultant when I produced the Phil Hellmuth poker DVDs. He was a solid player, which made him stand out in this crowd—and kind of go against what it was Tobey and I were trying to do here.

When I had asked Tobey about it, he'd done his trademark smirk and told me he'd allowed Andy to play on condition he funneled 50 percent of his winnings Tobey's way. We compared

Andy's play to a blue-chip stock. It wasn't gonna make ya rich, but he would maintain a slow and steady growth . . . and that was enough for Tobey. Sharp son of a bitch was working the angles even better than I was!

Stranger still is that I would later learn that Andy was one of the richest guys there: it turned out he's the heir to the friggin' Chiquita Banana fortune for Christ's sake. Andy would also be a key component as to why the game would eventually move out of The Viper Room and into next-level craziness.

That left three more players.

Commercial real estate magnate Bob Safi is known now for his appearances on the *Late Night Poker* show—he was actually asked to the show after we allowed the producer to sweat our game one night in an effort to try and recruit high-stakes players for the show. Bob was one of the guys who took them up on the offer along with hedge fund mogul Mike Baxter.

I loved playing cards with Bobby. Unlike his conservative play on television, when the cameras were off, he was an absolute stone-cold maniac. He made the game play super big, but at the same time, aside from me and Tobey, Bob was one of the few long-term winners in the game. Some of the biggest and best nights in my life were had with Bob Safi just a few seats away . . . and some of the most painful nights, as well.

Then there was Dylan Sellers, a B-movie producer whose career had never lived up to the promise of his early hit *Passenger 57*—although I think he later ended up at the Weinstein Company and made a huge turnaround for himself. Whether or not his poker game ever got turned around, I couldn't tell you.

Dylan was the kind of guy who loved gambling so much he would lie to his assistant and tell her he had an important meeting when really he was heading to the Commerce to play poker around two in the afternoon on a weekday. Dylan wasn't scared to get involved in a big pot, but in those days he usually lost. He was certainly one of the big losers that first night at the Viper.

The last guy to show up was Darin Feinstein, who owned the joint and who had fixed it for Molly to play hostess. One thing she did get right in her book: Darin was a loud, rude, and incredibly crude dude—and I liked him from the first time I met him.

He came in shouting, "Let's fuckin' do this, fools!" and we sat down to play . . . and from that moment it all went off like an episode of *MacGyver*!

Manny was there quietly doing his thing, and Molly, as well as taking drink orders, had put together the world's worst poker mix tape to play in the background. When Kenny Rogers's "The Gambler" came on, I think it was Todd who finally stepped up and said, "What the fuck?"

The whole table burst out laughing, and Molly—blushing the deepest scarlet—skipped to the next song, which was "Night Moves" by Bob Segar, and for some reason, we all loved it. There was a big pot that happened during that tune, and it became our game's theme song for a while.

And talking of big pots . . . from the start they were bigger than anything that happened in Tobey's kitchen.

The plan we had made about keeping the buy-ins low and the blinds high worked like a charm. Before the button had made one lap around the table, Parker and Brill were already reloading. In fact, they kept reloading and hitting the felt all night long.

As I looked around the table and sipped my diet raspberry Snapple iced tea and watched the game unfold, I was reminded of something from my childhood, back in the Midwest.

When I was a kid my parents got me the *Odyssey 2* video game console instead of the Atari 2600 because the guy at the Magnavox store (who coincidentally made the *Odyssey 2*) told them it was a better unit and was more "educational" because it had a computer keyboard attached to it.

To go with it they also bought me the *Odyssey* equivalent to *Pac Man*, which was called *KC Munchkin*. The cool thing about *KC Munchkin* was the fact that you could build your own maze. So, being a little advantage-loving bastard even back then, I set out to create a maze that would allow me to eat all the dots but block in all of the monsters, so they could never eat me, thus guaranteeing me a win every time I played. And it suddenly struck me that's exactly what we had done with this game. We set it up in a way that gave us such a huge edge that in the long run it was impossible for us to get beat.

That's what I was thinking as I looked around that table—of my rigged *KC Munchkin* maze. All the pieces had been set up for a guaranteed checkmate.

Here was Leonardo DiCaprio, smiling, glad-handing, turning on the charm and playing his ultraconservative game with my money, here was *The Hangover* director Todd Phillips cracking filthy jokes and making out like he could read every player in the room. Here were a few other Hollywood players, a producer, a director, and here were a couple of real estate millionaires, some kind of European aristocrat type, an heir to the Chiquita Banana fortune, the former CEO to Callaway Golf clubs . . . and here was Tobey, smiling to himself with that wicked little lopsided grin that some people found so charming and others so scary.

Here was Manny and the Shuffle Master, keeping things moving fast and efficiently; and here were the pots, stacking up behind those two-hundred-dollar blinds. Here was the Eurotrash guy reloading once, twice, three times; here was the former CEO of Callaway Golf and the heir to the Max Factor fortune following him.

Here was my stack of chips, steadily, inevitably, getting bigger.

And here, floating around, serving drinks, setting up snacks, counting cash, was Molly Bloom, making out like she was in charge of it all.

I could have laughed out loud. The Viper Room game was born . . . and I knew right then that this beautiful little Hollywood Heist we'd set up could only get bigger and crazier with every passing week.

By the time we called it a night, Leo had pretty well broken even, as we suspected; Bellin and Todd Phillips had both squeaked out meager wins; and Steve Brill, Dean Factor, and Bruce Parker got comprehensively buried. Unfortunately, so did Darin. I remember being bummed out for him—he lost a huge pot on a bad beat that night, and I was really hoping to see him win, being the host and all.

Last, Tobey and I both scored huge: I cashed out a smokin' seventy-eight grand richer than I had started the evening. It was the biggest single night of my life thus far. And as I drove home in a weird, wired daze of adrenaline and dog-tiredness, all I kept thinking was . . . this was only the beginning. Seventy-eight thousand big ones—and this was just the first night. Holy crap!

And man was I right. The fish were hooked; week after week, they would come swimming back for more. And week after week Tobey and I would reel them in. It got to be almost surreal: for example, Bruce Parker was always good for about thirty grand, after which he would shut it down for the night. And to us that seemed like sensible, conservative play . . . which just goes to show how fucked up things were getting. In what world would someone who dropped $30k every week and then bowed out, dignity intact, be seen as an exemplar of restraint?

But compared to a few of the other guys, Parker was a nun. For some, there was no stop button . . . only full steam ahead, regardless of the cost. Remember Kevin Washington? The son of the Montana billionaire who would spit chew in a cup when we was playing in Tobey's kitchen? He was something else entirely.

Talk about hitting the genetic lottery. Kevin was about 6'5" and built like a brick shithouse. He looked like a movie star and had more money than he could ever spend. Not that he didn't try, of course. God knows he threw enough of it our way. And it seemed the only thing he loved more than losing at poker was getting loaded while he did it.

I'll never forget meeting up with Kevin to get paid the day after one of our many big games. He was having a champagne brunch in the polo lounge with a supermodel. I showed up to get paid, and he handed me a fifty-thousand-dollar brick of cash right there in the restaurant. You could see the girl's eyes following the money all the way from Kevin's hand into mine and then up to see me smiling like the cat that got the canary. Just for the fun of it I decided to give her a wink as I walked out. Damn that was fun.

On another night, Kevin went off the rails for a clear hundred grand and was simply too drunk to drive after the game. Since I was the one who had reaped the benefit of his drunkenness the most, I volunteered to help get him to wherever he needed to go.

I cashed out and had Kevin leave his brand-new Viper in the parking lot and hop in my new $200,000 Mercedes (I felt like pointing out he'd pretty much paid for it but decided it was best not to rub the guy's nose in it), and I asked him where he lived. It was then he decided he was hungry and wanted to go to Mel's Diner on Sunset. Mel's is this famous all-night diner that's been around forever. People would pile in after the clubs closed every night in the hope of seeing a wasted celeb or two chowing down on a burger . . . and the thing is, a lot of the time they would, too. One time me and my buddy Rick Mahr tipped the door guy a C-note to get seated ahead of a young Chris Hemsworth, who sat there waiting for a table wondering who in the hell we were.

Kevin and I sat down, and he literally ordered every breakfast and side item on the menu. Our table was packed with pancakes, waffles, omelets, bacon, eggs, you name it . . . and our man here was dive-bombing Mozzarella sticks into his ketchup and making airplane sounds like a little kid. And if that wasn't weird, once he calmed down he turned maudlin, and that was even weirder.

The more he ate, the more serious his tone became. Before we left he was complaining how his brother was the golden child and could do no wrong in the eyes of the world. He claimed his brother could snort a giant line of blow and then go break a world ski jump record, and how unfair it was, how his father was so much more proud of him, how hard it was being the son of Dennis Washington, how much he was gonna regret having to answer to him about blowing his monthly allowance . . .

And all I could think was: are you fucking kidding me? I mean, I guess money can't always buy happiness for everyone, but even still, it was pretty damn hard to feel sorry for him. At that point Kevin was on a $250k per month allowance from his father but would inherit billions when he turned thirty.

It got even more surreal.

After we left Mel's, Kevin directed me up a dozen little winding streets through the Hollywood Hills. I thought I was driving him home to sleep it off, but as we pulled up to his place there was a limo waiting with its engine running and a driver standing outside the door. Kev was going home alright—back to Montana for the night. In his private jet.

I asked how he knew the driver would be waiting, and he told me he was instructed to have the car running and to wait there all night until Kevin returned. Unreal.

A few weeks later, Darin Feinstein told us that Kevin was arrested while in France and thrown into a French prison for making some kind of drunken racial slur in a bar. (I have no idea if the story was true.) According to his version of events, he eventually got bailed out by the prince of some third-world country. What a life this guy had. One time he sent Darin a video from his phone that had all of these Colombian girls naked on their knees cleaning the floor of his yacht to the tune of the 1970s disco hit "Car Wash" by Rose Royce. You see that kind of shit and believe me, you feel a whole lot less bad about hustling him for a hundred grand every now and then.

Even as Tobey and I took guys like Kevin Washington, Bruce Parker, and Dean Factor to the cleaners every week, it seemed every rich wannabe in LA was queuing to be next to lose money to us. From *Girls Gone Wild* creator Joe Francis, who didn't know the difference between a straight and a flush, to oil heir Brandon Davis, who was always half in the bag, there wasn't a rich guy who loved to gamble who didn't try to make his way into our game! The waiting list could have earned its own issue of *Forbes* called "The World's Richest Suckers"! The game was quickly becoming the most talked-about secret on the Sunset Strip. And while it was the hottest ticket for the in-crowd, it was also, silently, discreetly, making me rich.

The thing you have to remember is, for the millionaires and billionaires around that table, the major Hollywood bigwigs, the A-list celebs, the heirs to fortunes and owners of empires, it was all just good fun. But I was different. The game was quickly becoming a true source of revenue for me that would quickly rival the day job of being a producer in Hollywood.

Sure, I was making money now—a lot of money, more money than I could have imagined a decade or two earlier—but whatever kind of safety net I had was significantly more threadbare than anyone else's in the game. A guy like Kevin Washington could shrug off back-to-back six-figure losses, blow another grand on breakfast, and then hop in his private jet to Montana and forget about it all by the morning . . . and I most certainly could not.

I still had bills to pay. I was making money hand over fist—but all it would take was one really bad run and I'd be drowning in shit creek . . . without paddle, boat, life jacket, or even swimming trunks to speak of. And so, conscious not to put all my eggs in one basket—but also because a hustler's gonna hustle—I decided to spread my action around a bit.

By the time we started playing at The Viper Room, my life was getting pretty damn busy. My company, Big Vision Entertainment, was taking off, and I was in preproduction on a couple of TV pilots . . . and in addition to my gig with Tobey, I was also playing in a bunch of other games throughout the week. They may not have had the edge of the Viper games, but they each had their own appeal.

There was a dealer's choice game operating out of a garage in Glendale that was mobbed up with Armenians. It was run by this dude named Arman. I called him Arman the Angle Shooter, because he was always trying to shoot some kind of dirty scumbag angle at the table. The only reason I even played with these guys was that they had a couple of doctors in the game with deep pockets and everyone took turns dealing, which meant I got to keep my mechanics sharp. I also had a silent partner in the game who I would deal most of our big winning hands to, which allowed the appearance of me being a loose cannon, as I would siphon off my entire stack to my partner by the end of the night along with everyone else's money. All they seemed to remember was me dumping chips, which is exactly what I intended. But aside from all that, they liked having me there mostly because they were always hoping I would invite them to the Viper . . . which was never going to happen.

Although strangely, one of the fish from that game ended up at the Viper anyway, through Darin. Everyone called him "The Rug Merchant," which mystified me until I had to pick up a check from him one day for twenty-seven grand, and the address he gave led to his family's Persian rug store. I would later find out they were the largest importer of designer rugs in the country.

Aside from the Rug Merchant and the doctors, the majority of these guys were all piss-poor cheaters and wannabe scam artists, so I had no qualms about taking their dough.

The ballsiest thing I ever did in their game (or any game perhaps) was the time we were seven-handed and I rang in a cooler. A cooler or cold deck is a deck that has been stacked to deliver a desired outcome. To switch a deck in play for a cooler on the fly takes a lot of skill and a pair of balls that would make King Kong feel inferior. A deck switch is one of the hardest sleight-of-hand moves to execute in fast company . . . and I don't mind telling you, one of the craziest, too. In fact, it is a move that is almost done exclusively when working with several partners who are looking to take down a single mark. But I did it with only one ally! It doesn't bear thinking about what they might have done to me if they had caught me.

I had prestacked the hidden cooler in a way that would generate action from the entire table. When the dealer offered me the cut, I secretly made the switch in the act of cutting the cards, and the whole thing played out just as it was supposed to. It's worth reiterating the fact that I made the switch while being offered to cut the deck as opposed to doing it during my own deal. Therefore the cooler hand was dealt by the player to my left (who was one of the marks I was taking down), leaving myself in the clear as soon as the switch occurred. I have since named the stacking procedure the "St. Valentine's Day Massacre" in honor of the famed seven-man mob hit in Chicago that stemmed out of the feud between Al Capone and Bugs Moran. My starting hand was the worst at the table—a king and a ten of clubs. By the turn, everyone was all-in. And with the river came the sweet smell of a family pot victory. It was the kind of hand reserved for movies like *The Sting* or perhaps a Scorsese flick!

The action of this hand was so over-the-top ridiculous that no one would ever suspect it of being stacked. I busted the entire table that night (aside from my partner) and never went back to the game again. Am I worried these guys will come after me when they read this? Nah. Fuck 'em. They were robbing everyone they played with, they deserved to go broke! Plus, their egos were so huge they would hate to admit that someone got one over on them.

The Armenians played on Saturdays. On Monday it was industry night at famed producer Jon Landau's house—a game that I was turned on to by Jon Moonves, who also got me a spot at Nick Cassavetes's game, which was always filled with ruthless late-night all-in play. Landau's game was low stakes by comparison and more of an industry get-together. I never focused on busting that game, because that was not the purpose it served. But Cassavetes's game was pretty damn serious.

Cassavetes was Hollywood royalty. His mother was Gena Rowlands, and his father was the famed director John Cassavetes, who helped to pioneer the independent film genre. Right in line with his Greek heritage, Nick lived atop Mt. Olympus, a sprawling Hollywood Hills neighborhood that was home to dozens of big-league entertainment industry types. Nick's game was on Wednesdays and first started in his garage, then later moved into his house.

It seemed that every time I went to Nick's the house was under construction. He was always changing stuff around: a wall would be dark red one week, dark blue the next, and the week after that it wouldn't even be there at all.

Playing at Nick's always felt like I was living in a scene from *Goodfellas* meets *Entourage* (which was kind of funny, as he later appeared in that show). Nick modified everyone's name to fit the vibe he was putting out. There was Chuck whom he called Chucky, Frank was Franky, Moonves was "Jonny Moon," Rick Salomon of Paris Hilton–filming fame was of course "Scum," which suited him pretty well, and he always called me "Housty."

It gave the game a nicely shady feel, which I loved. Hell, I thrived on it. Nick didn't believe in all of the pomp and circumstance Spidey and I had to use to lure our prey into the net. At his house it was Mexican food from Paquito Mos, and his girlfriend, Queeny, would deal. He encouraged us to tip Queeny, which probably ended up making him an extra five grand per night on top of everything else. And there were plenty of side bets going on, which allowed for some shrewd hustling.

Oil heir Brandon Davis showed up plastered—he was early and Nick and I were the only people there, but Brandon was desperate to get going straightaway. Nick pulled me aside and asked if I wouldn't mind helping him chop the kid up. I thought, sure, why not.

I was dealing, which made it a lock. We all put in ten grand for a freeze-out. In the second hand, Nick dumped all of his chips to me and gave me a wink. Meanwhile, he poured Brandon another shot of Jack Daniels. I didn't waste any time. I could beat the kid straight up any day of the week, but I couldn't be bothered wasting the mental energy. So I riffle-stacked a double duke and four hands in dealt him pocket jacks. Naturally he got all-in . . . and I turned over a pair of queens. Just to add insult to injury, I flopped a set and rivered a boat.

Nick was in a great mood that night due to the fact that we'd cleaned Brandon out before the actual game even started, but in truth I actually felt sorry for the kid. He had grown up with everything he ever wanted, yet his soul just seemed empty. Weeks later, Brandon would be bringing over expensive paintings to try and pay off his gambling debts. Not to mention, he was always sweating profusely and shaking for some reason. He always looked like a junkie who was on his second day of rehab.

Every time I saw Brandon outside of the game, he always seemed to remember me, which was surprising considering he was rarely sober. On three occasions he wanted to show me a picture of the model he was dating on his phone. He was a wild kid in his twenties, hanging out with Mischa Barton and Paris

Hilton. Hell, he's the guy who nicknamed Lindsay Lohan "fire crotch" . . . to the outside world he had it all . . . but I'm not sure he was ever truly happy.

One time I met with him at the Polo Lounge, and he pitched me a show idea. It was gonna be a reality show with him going around the country, finding bums and people down on their luck and then giving them a big wad of cash to see how fast they would blow it. He thought it was hilarious. I later heard he got into art in a big way.

I didn't play every week at Cassavetes's game. There was an unwritten rule at Nick's, if you wanted to play you had to "earn" your seat . . . and that meant dumping a few big hands to Nick throughout the night. The rule was never spoken, but Nick knew how to make you feel it, believe me.

A lot of guys got intimidated by Nick. After all, he was about 6'5" and had a giant skull and crossbones tattooed across his entire fucking chest. I got to where I was making so much money with Tobey in our game that I just flat out refused to play soft at Nick's. Sure enough, it didn't take long before I was reduced to the "standby" list.

But despite that, every time Nick and I saw each other it was all smiles and fist bumps. He was just an exciting and fun guy to be around, and there was always something crazy happening at his place. I'll never forget the time one of the players had left the table to meet a friend. A minute later my cell rang, and I stepped out in the garage to take the call in private.

When I got out there I saw this dude who had showed up in a Prius carrying what appeared to be a giant fishing tackle box. He opened it, and not only did he have a shit ton of weed in there, but the box was also packed with coke, speed, painkillers, and enough pills and powder to fell an elephant . . . as well as a huge bag of what I assume must have been heroin. He was not fucking around.

The funny thing is, the cat who had called him just wanted to buy a few Xanax. But this dealer was prepared to cater for every taste, and in Hollywood, there is always someone ready to give you whatever you want, whenever you want it, as long as you've got the money.

Anyway: back to business. Between Saturday night with the Armenians, Monday at Jon Landau's house, Tuesdays with Tobey at The Viper Room and Wednesday at Cassavetes's, my poker schedule was getting pretty full. And I still had the Thursday pot limit game in Beverly Hills run by Asher Dan and his cronies plus the occasional Hank Azaria game whenever he was in town.

But one by one, they all began to lose their luster—all except for The Viper Room game. It not only had the best action by far, but Tobey and I were perfecting the heist down to a science—and we were getting a good stream of players to dump some decent dough.

It was also fun as hell—and you never knew what kind of surprises might occur.

CHAPTER 5

MONEY TALKS, BULLSHIT WALKS

Our game had become bigger than I could have imagined—or hoped for. Huge names were coming every week, and in addition to providing action, they'd often bring a buddy or a girlfriend or two to come watch as Hollywood's elite won or lost (although they mostly lost) tens of thousands of dollars on the turn of every street.

From Tobey and Leo to *The Hangover* director Todd Phillips, *Mighty Ducks* director Steve Brill, Joe Francis, Dean Factor (the heir to the Max Factor fortune), Madonna's record label chief whiz kid Guy Oseary, to CEOs and winners of the rich kid genetic lottery, we had become Tinseltown's hottest ticket by far. After more and more people started hearing about the star-studded game happening in the bowels of The Viper Room, security began to become a concern. Sure, we couldn't turn away an A-list buddy of Leo's who wanted to see what the noise was about, or a couple of bimbos hanging on the arms of Rick Salomon (and in truth girls like those at least brightened the place up), but given the clientele—and the sheer amount of money involved—keeping the man on the door alert was a must.

With that in mind I would tip our gatekeeper a C-note every week. Many of the other regulars did, too. Why? Let's just say it made doubly sure that guy always had our back.

Then there was the hostess with the stamp; she got tipped, too. Don't underestimate the power of a girl with a handstamp! Even if some rounder managed to make it past our man at the door, he'd be hard-pressed to get through her.

And then to top it off Darin was always packing a gun. He didn't exactly advertise the fact, but I knew, because I was pretty observant when it came to stuff like that. Thank Christ he never felt he had to use it.

The result of all this was that our security was tight. One night, pro poker player Layne Flak tried to penetrate the game by showing up with a bag of cash and got turned away at the door, flat out. It saved an awkward scene . . . and most likely saved me and Tobey a few thousand dollars, too. Not that Lane would have won it from us, but he would have won it from our fish, which is basically the same thing.

However, sometimes it worked a little too well.

One time Tobey phoned his girlfriend Jen from the game—he'd left home in a rush that night and forgot to bring his vegan dinner. (I know—rock 'n' roll, huh?) So Jen agreed to bring it by but after an hour still hadn't showed. All of a sudden Tobey's cell starts buzzing: on the line was a very upset Jen screaming at Spider-Man that the bouncer just told her the only way she was gonna be let in the door was if she got on her knees and blew him. Oh Fuck!

We sent Molly to sort out the situation, and Darin followed her, ready to chew this guy's ass out. Meanwhile Tobey looks and me with wide eyes and says: "Fuck, does this mean I've gotta go fight this dude?"

When the doorman came back in, he was holding a dozen red roses he must have bought at the corner market, got on his knees, professed how deeply sorry he was to Jen, and then swore to her and everyone in the room that he was secretly gay and was just trying to protect the privacy of the game at all cost.

You could have heard a pin drop . . . before everyone started laughing, Tobey slapped him on the back, and what could have been a tricky situation was nipped in the bud.

It gave me a new level of respect for Darin because I knew that was entirely his way of saving face for The Viper Room—and it worked. Tobey was off the hook, Jen was satisfied, and we went back to making it rain. Hell, the guy even got his usual C-note at the end of the night.

Fun and games aside, we were still in the business of making as much money off as many suckers as possible. Our goal was to always be finding bigger fish. But while I was more than happy with the Bruce Parkers and Kevin Washingtons of this world, Tobey had bigger ambitions. He wasn't going to rest until he'd landed Moby fuckin' Dick. He wanted players who were insanely rich, had no cap, and weren't dependent on Daddy's money to write a big check. Enter Alec Gores!

Alec was a Lebanese Catholic from Israel who moved to the United States when he was 15 and got a job bagging groceries for his uncle's store in Flint, Michigan. He didn't bag groceries for long: before he was in his thirties, he and his kid brother Tom had both become self-made billionaires as leverage buy-out geniuses. And the third brother, Sam Gores, owns Paradigm, one of the premier talent agencies in the entertainment business.

At that time this cat was worth around $1.3 billion, and *Forbes* had him marked as the 606th richest person in the entire god-damn world. So when Tobey had somehow run into him at a party somewhere, he naturally invited him to play.

One of the famous stories I had heard about Alec was when he hired famed Hollywood private investigator Anthony Pellicano to find out if his wife Lisa was sleeping around behind his back. The bad news was that his suspicions were right, Lisa was seeing someone else. The really bad news was that someone else was little brother Tom.

How fucked up is that? But the real kicker is that it didn't seem to have affected their relationship—because from what I knew they were still close. That's Alec and Tom, not the ex-wife—he divorced her quicker than you can say "prenup."

That was all history by the time he joined our game, and Alec was very much free and single again—and making the most of it, too. The first night he played at the Viper, he showed up with this hot young thing on his arm . . . as well as one of the Olsen twins, who just happened to be BFFs with Alec's new squeeze.

Also playing that night was Joe Francis, who had made his millions from the *Girls Gone Wild* video franchise. Joe and I had known each other for a while because my *Backyard Wrestling* videos gave him a run for his money when we started buying up a lot of his ad time.

He was also a certified total douchebag. I had a meeting with him once, and the first thing he said to me was "Have you received a letter from my attorney yet?" I asked him what he was talking about, and he told me he was planning on suing me for using the phrase "banned from television" in my ad. After I stopped laughing and was ready to leave the meeting, he started making a play to get my retail distribution. That's Joe for ya.

So, in walks Alec with his girl of the week and Mary Kate Olsen of the Olsen twins, and immediately Joe Francis sprung up and was all: "Hey there babe, how are ya?"

She looked at Joe and with the utmost sincerity said, "Have we met?"

This sent Joe into a rage. Without hesitation he shouted: "Well you sure remembered my name when you were snorting blow off my cock in the back of my limo!"

The room went more dead silent than the time Tobey's girlfriend had accused the doorman of propositioning her for a blow job. Even Manny stopped dealing the cards. And then, in the total silence, out of nowhere, Tobey could no longer hold it together and burst out laughing. Within a few seconds the whole room was howling . . . and the Olsen girl left superpissed. Instead of denying it and calling Joe a liar (which anyone would have believed based on his criminal history with women) she just got upset and left.

Alec dumped a small fortune that night. I remember watching him closely and noticed that he was approaching the game differently from everyone else. Players generally fall into two camps: those who are playing because they want to win money, and those who are playing simply because they love gambling, win or lose. Alec was different.

As the night went on I got the unshakable feeling he was studying the game for the long haul and was willing to make a major investment in order to learn how to beat our play down the road—like a kind of loss leader in business.

Interesting . . . though ultimately it was never going to pay off for him, of course, at least not on my watch. Plus, Tobey and I knew that Alec could potentially write off millions while learning to play good poker, and that could only be good for us—and good for the game in general.

And of course Alec Gores was not the only fish in the sea. We were landing them at a sweet and steady rate now. Another one of the marks we recruited was a man named Larry Haun. Larry was an older guy who had a wife less than half his age and owned a huge gaudy-looking house in Beverly Hills that was loaded with cold marble floors and tons of gold.

He was worth about 300 million dollars, and he made every penny of it selling knock-off perfume. You know all those hawkers that come up to you on the street in New York and say, "Hey, if your wife likes Chanel 5, then she'll love this"? That was basically Larry's brainchild. Larry had the business set up like a multilevel marketing scheme where he ended up making three dollars off every bottle sold! Every week I would ask him how many bottles he moved, and it was always between 50 and 100,000 units! That's a lot of cheap perfume!

Todd Phillips would always call Larry "Old Spice" and would tell him his place looked like Uday Hussein's house, which was both funny and kinda true. Larry felt doubly insulted that Todd chose Uday instead of his father, Saddam Hussein. . . . which is exactly what Todd intended to do. It's safe to say that Larry fucking hated Todd. What made it worse is that Todd would always threaten to sleep with Larry's hot young wife. Larry got really upset by it, but damn it cracked the rest of us up: "Hey Old Spice, I really think I'm gonna fuck your wife tonight . . . you wouldn't mind, would ya?" It was awful, but truly hilarious.

I gotta hand it to Larry, though. He lost money like a true gentleman, like losing money was the whole reason he was there in the first place (which of course it was, but only Tobey and I were supposed to know that). Even when Larry won, he would find a way to politely give it back. One time he rivered producer Chuck Pacheco out of a pot for about thirty grand, and when he saw how upset Chuck was, he just shrugged and handed it back to him. Chuck turned to me and said, "Look, Larry just gave me a fucking Prius!"

He would also tip Molly and Manny thousands of dollars whether he won or lost. They loved him for that, of course . . . and for my part I never felt bad taking Larry's money, simply because I knew he would never run out.

I also liked the guy. I once asked him if he could send my mom a bottle of his best fake perfume, and without hesitation he asked for her address and overnighted her a giant case with every knock-off he made. Old Spice was a good man.

The last time I saw Larry he had just bought his hot young wife a huge new mansion that sat on a giant horse ranch in Calabasas. I heard she left him right after that. Poor bastard. Still, it's hard to feel too sorry for a guy who makes hundreds of millions of dollars peddling fake perfume . . .

It was an electrifying time in my life. Tuesdays at The Viper Room had easily become my favorite night of the week—and while we were taking care of business downstairs, the joint was beginning to rock again upstairs, too. Which of course made walking through the lines getting the VIP treatment with all the cool kids of LA wondering who you were even more fun than it had been before.

Every week for a long time this awesome rock band was playing upstairs. I would later learn it was Grammy-nominated Cisco Adler and one of his early bands. I remember one of the guys in the game had a smokin' hot girlfriend he would bring with him every Tuesday—and while he was downstairs lining my pockets, she would be upstairs getting bottle service and partying to Cisco like there was no tomorrow . . . most likely with every eye in the place on her.

Tobey and I had become tighter than ever. Why wouldn't we be? Things could not have been going better. From a chance meeting at the Commerce and a set of scratch games in his kitchen to creating the hottest hustle in Hollywood—we'd come a long way, baby! And not only were we raking in insane amounts of cash every week, we had LA's richest whales queuing up for the privilege of handing over their mad money to us. Life was sweet. Whatever else came to pass, those days were golden.

On top of everything else, my career was steadily on the rise. I had just signed with ICM and was starting a new TV project called *The Ultimate Blackjack Tour* on CBS. It was more than just a show, it was a new online gaming business venture. I was in preproduction and partnered up with Jon Moonves and former WSOP champion Russ Hamilton (who had cofounded UltimateBet.com)—as well as a talented young entrepreneur named Kasey Thompson.

Kasey was the son of a lawyer who had settled one of the biggest tobacco class-action lawsuits in the country. His brother was a top surgeon at the Mayo Clinic (who ironically was also named Houston), and Kasey was the founder of a poker magazine called *All-In*. Now there was a phrase that was going to come back to haunt him . . .

Kasey was quickly becoming famous among those in the high-stakes poker world for being a maniac gambler—I saw him once play in the big game at the Bellagio with his cards FACE UP on the table! He was also a serious drinker back then. He had decided to stop by the game one night while three sheets to the wind, so I waited for my moment and decided this was the night I was going to have the biggest win of my life.

It took a while, but I finally got in a hand with Kasey with pocket sixes and the flop came 5, 6, 5. Sweet: I had flopped a boat, and Kasey was betting into me like a madman.

I smooth called a twenty-thousand-dollar bet on the flop, and the turn peeled off a ten. Kasey drunkenly pushed all of his chips in the pot. Gotcha!

I called. The river showed another 10 and for a moment I worried that maybe he backed into a miracle runner full house . . . but then Kasey said, "Nope, you got it!" and drunkenly tossed his hand into the muck.

As his cards bounced on the table, they accidentally turned over. He was holding a deuce and a ten. He had just rivered me for a hundred grand, and he didn't even know it!

Tobey immediately began laughing at my pain. We both liked to rib each other whenever one of us took a bad beat. I felt genuinely ill over it. My first six-figure takedown had just turned into a six-figure loss. That's how brutal poker can be when you aren't in control of the cards! I was superbummed, but I figured I'd get the money back eventually, and what the hell, it will be good for the game in the long run. Kasey also took director Steve Brill for a small fortune that night—and Steve was out for blood. Even though he and I weren't that close, Brill approached me outside and asked if I would help him lure Kasey over to his house to continue playing so we could win our money back. Hmmm, a pass-the-deal home game with a drunken rich guy . . . I was in.

So Steve, Kasey and I, plus a couple of Kasey's buddies, all trooped up to Brill's house after the game—and with me taking on dealing duties it was a blowout. I made Steve a nice chunk of change, got more than my hundred grand back, and the night ended with Kasey throwing up in Brill's toilet barely able to walk.

To be fair to the guy, he met me the next day at the Mondrian hotel off Sunset with a trash bag full of cash to pay his debt. God Bless America!

But that still wasn't the end of our adventures with Kasey. For starters, Kasey and I went into business together producing *The Ultimate Blackjack Tour* on CBS along with WSOP champ Russ Hamilton. More on that later. Not long after our all-nighter at Brill's house, there was a major tournament happening in Vegas—a $15k buy-in head-up tourney. Given the roll we were on, Spidey called me up and said: "I'm taking a private jet to Vegas, are you in?" Hell yeah I was in!

There were six of us on that jet, and I remember nobody even offered to pitch in on the cost except me. I guess everyone figured Tobey would just cover it. I think he appreciated the fact that I never assumed anything when it came to money—and God knows I could afford it. I was rolling in cash by that point.

As the plane took off, Tobey and Jen held hands and then reached for the hand of whoever was sitting next to them. It was a ritual, that they all hold hands whenever taking off in a private jet. Despite the fact that we were being served hors d'oeuvres in the lap of luxury . . . the hand-holding thing kinda gave me a warm, spiritual feeling . . . something I rarely had when on my way to Sin City.

When we landed it was like a scene right out of a movie. As we walked off our private jet and sauntered across the runway to a waiting stretch limousine waiting to take us to our luxury suites at the Mirage, Tobey turned to me and said, "Are you feeling like a rock star yet?" We laughed all the way to the casino.

Due to the $15k buy-in, the tournament was basically all pros—a far cry from our easy pickings at The Viper Room. Tobey got stuck playing heads up with the legendary TJ Cloutier, the guy who has probably made more final tables than any other player in history and the author of several books on poker strategy. I ended up playing against Freddy Deeb. Freddy was also a pro and a hell of a player: we already knew each other because he was one of the players on my *Ultimate Blackjack Tour* TV show.

The tournament was a three-game structure: whoever won two out of three freeze-outs would advance.

Tobey lost two in a row to TJ, and I remember busting his balls about it. He told me the guy wouldn't shut up the entire time and how it was so damn nerve-rattling to play with him. I beat Freddy on my first freeze-out, he beat me on the second one . . . and then after he got me on the third, our tournament was over.

Did that mean it was time to go home? Don't be ridiculous. It was time to go to work. Tobey hated to lose as much as I did, so we set out on a fishing expedition.

We headed over to the Bellagio and began scouting out the big games, and suddenly I saw a wave of happiness come over Tobey's face, like the sun emerging from behind a dark cloud. Right there in Bobby's Room at the Bellagio, at the high-limit table surrounded by legendary pros like Doyle Brunson, Phil Ivey, and Jennifer Harmon, was none other than Kasey Thompson. His cards were face up and his nose was wide open.

Tobey was bouncing now. "Go convince Kasey to quit dumping his money and come hang out with us," he told me. Which was code for . . . get him away from those professionals so he can throw his money at us instead.

Ten minutes later it was just me, Tobey, and Kasey alone in my villa. I have to admit that for perhaps the first time since we had formed our plan to take down the richest marks in Hollywood, I was very torn about this. I knew the goal was to bust Kasey, but the fact was, while Tobey was my so-called partner in crime, Kasey was my actual business partner on the UBT. Plus the fact it was just the three of us alone in my suite with a bottle of booze and a deck of cards made it feel less like a game of poker and more like we were about to roll a drunk. The kid wouldn't stand a chance.

Tobey wanted to play freeze-outs for fifty grand a pop. I politely declined, figuring that was the smart thing to do, but that just made it harder because then they asked me to deal.

I knew I didn't need to use any mechanics to help Tobey win, considering how good he was and how drunk Kasey was, but I didn't know if I would be able to help myself. And then after Tobey had won three $50k freeze-outs in a row, Kasey said something that made Tobey light up while at the same time giving me a sinking feeling in my stomach for Kasey.

"Hey Tobe," he shouted, "let's do one for a quarter nizzle!"

That's "nizzle" as in "million." Holy fuck. Kasey wanted to play for $250k against a guy who had just beat him three times in a row.

At this point the shit had got seriously real. Before I knew it, Tobey was up $750k on Kasey. It was truly sick.

But Kasey, as drunk as he was, calmly asked Tobey to play for another $250k.

I couldn't watch Tobey beat him again. I figured it was time for Kasey to get lucky. He could knock off $250k of what he already owed Tobey, Tobey would still go home with over half a million bucks, and everyone would be happy. So I riffle-stacked Kasey pocket aces, which is always the best starting hand in Hold'em but is even more powerful when playing heads up. Tobey had won plenty, and I really wanted to help Kasey get some of his money back. The problem is, Kasey slow-played the aces so drunkenly that he allowed Tobey to flop an open-ender. Tobey was leading the action for once betting into Kasey, who, instead of raising like he would usually do, was just smooth-calling, which allowed Tobey to make his straight with very little risk. Of course after Kasey had the worst of it, he finally stuck all of his money in and Tobey drove the nail in the coffin.

I felt really bad for Kasey. He was down a million bucks and didn't even know what hit him. He dragged himself out of the room looking like he wanted to drive off a cliff, while Spider-Man, who was completely energized even after being up all night, dragged me to the gym with him and we worked out with his private trainer, who had flown into Vegas with us along with Tobey's chef.

What a crazy night. What a crazy life.

There's a postscript to this story—and one that maybe shows a different side to Tobey Maguire. A few weeks after our Vegas trip, Kasey, always as good as his word, met up with Tobey to pay him the million.

Tobey not only refused to take his money, but he also convinced Kasey to attend an AA class with him. And what makes the story even better is the fact that Tobey never even told me about it. Kasey did. Tobey didn't want to make a big deal out of doing something nice. He knew his life was blessed, and despite what some would have you believe, he has a truly good heart.

Not only did he turn down a million bucks, but he helped Kasey turn his life around . . . and he did it all under the radar. Hell, that's got me beat on my most generous day doing anything for anyone. Tobey earned a new level of my respect from me that day, yet the two of us have never even talked about it.

You won't hear any stories like that from Molly Bloom, that's for sure.

As time passed, and the pots kept getting bigger and bigger, Tuesday nights at The Viper Room felt like holding a golden lotto ticket that paid out every single week. And best of all, all the different elements of our plan were working together perfectly.

It was out of Tobey's house, so he didn't have to sweat any heat, and we had been dealing directly with Molly regarding the player lineup. (She later claimed to have been recruiting the whales herself, but nobody sat at our table without Tobey's say-so, and my consultation. Controlling who played was crucial to the heist.)

We were also having Molly run around the day after the game to collect from the losers and pay the winners. The amounts were getting so big that we had stopped using cash at the table and told everyone to bring a checkbook or settle up the next day, simply because all the rebuys were making the sheer amount of money involved borderline crazy—and with word spreading about the size of our action, our dude on the door was getting nervous about trouble. I'll never forget the time this dude lost $50k to me and tried to get me to fill out a W9 to get paid.

Then one day, things shifted. Out of the blue, our buddy Andy Bellin called and asked if we could have the game at his house that night. Sure, Tobey shrugged, why not? We had no idea at the time, but from that moment our days at The Viper Room would be over . . . and what was to come next would take the operation to a whole new level of outrageous excess.

CHAPTER 6

MOLLY'S GAME

Andy Bellin lived in the heart of the Hollywood Hills not so far from Tobey. His home looked like something out of the Golden Age of Hollywood—real old-school Sunset Boulevard type opulence. He knew it, too—the first time I ever went there Andy gave me a tour of its rich Hollywood history . . . I only wish I'd paid proper attention at the time.

Andy always downplayed his upper-class background—not only was he the heir to the Chiquita Banana fortune, his father was one of the most highly regarded plastic surgeons in New York. But then he wasn't one of those people who was happy to live off his family's wealth or reputation, and that's one of the things I liked about him: he was an operator in his own right, he blazed his own trail.

Plus, he was smart. I mean: whip smart. And most of all, he loved poker.

A former astrophysics major, he dropped out of college to play cards in shady clubs in New York when poker—or the kind we play anyway—was still a pretty much underground activity. And on top of this Andy had big aspirations as a writer, combining those two passions in his 2002 book, *Poker Nation*, and since racking up quite a string of credits as a screenwriter, including *Trust* in 2010 and *Lovelace* in 2013. He also consulted with me on a few poker instructional DVDs with Phil Hellmuth.

I got on really well with Andy—but I was under no illusion that we were from anything like the same worlds.

I remember in 2006 Andy invited myself and a select group of his LA friends to his lavish wedding to Texas socialite Katherine Lane Farish Criner in Houston.

To the best of my recollection, it was myself, Moonves, Landau, as well as our buddy Chris Williams (who is now a new media super mogul). Out of the four of us who flew in from LA, I was the only non-Jewish cat in the group. I'll never forget us all looking out of the window of the Houston Country Club and seeing George Bush Senior and former First Lady Barbara sipping mimosas in the Texas sun. I believe it was Landau who turned to Moonves, Williams, and me and drawled: "I think we're outnumbered, boys."

But I'm getting ahead of myself: all that was still a long way off from the night Molly convinced Andy to invite us to play at his house instead of the Viper Room. Tobey and I had been wondering exactly why the game was suddenly switching locations—not only had The Viper proved a lucrative venue for us, its vibe was that sweet combination of glamorous and sleazy that felt perfect for the game—but it didn't take long for us to find out.

As soon as we got there, Andy spilled the beans.

It turns out Andy had been getting a little side action with Molly all of his own, and in the course of their extracurricular shenanigans, she had revealed to him that Darin was threatening to take the game away from her.

You've gotta give the girl credit: she could work a hand as well as any of us. Of course, in the movie, when Darin's character "Dean" accuses Molly of sleeping around with his friends, Jessica Chastain portrays Molly passionately denying the accusation.

That was all complete horseshit, naturally. Molly knew exactly what she was doing—and she knew that, handled right, Andy could help her turn things back around on Darin and secure the game for herself. Then again, it wasn't like she was doing anything illegal, or even immoral, by today's standards. They were both young and single living it up in Tinseltown. She had an ace down her skirt and she played it beautifully. Hell, you can't fault her for it . . . even if you do think it's pretty shitty not to fess up to any of her own shortcomings while trashing practically everyone else through her memoirs.

I remember the time she told me how she caught a glimpse of Andy's checking account from a bank statement lying on his desk and saw a recent deposit for nine million dollars. She had a great catch with Andy, but she screwed it up. Soon after that night, Andy walked in on her sleeping with her ex and dropped her like a sack of bad Chiquita bananas. I think they remained friends afterward . . . but Andy moved back to New York soon after and had nothing to do with the big game from that point on.

So there we were: out of The Viper Room, temporarily set up at Andy's place, and, so Molly would have us believe at least, under new management. What did that mean for me and Tobey? It meant a new angle to work, of course!

Ever the man with an eye for the bigger picture, Tobey saw this as a great time to get Molly under his thumb even more. Far from it being the moment Molly took control, it was the moment Tobey let her know who was really the Alpha Dog.

That night, Spidey explained to her in no uncertain terms that if she wanted to hold on to the game, she was gonna have to work for it. And that didn't just mean calling us all up to remind us about the game, serve a few drinks, and put together corny poker playlists on her iPod. We wanted her to take charge of the bank, seek out new fish, find a variety of five-star hotels to host us every week, lay on whatever other extras the players demanded . . . and take the cost of it all out of her ridiculous tips. And of course she was so nervous about losing her place on the lucrative roller-coaster ride she'd found herself on—and the fast, easy, glitzy cash that came with it—she said yes to everything.

Last, and with that creeping, deceptively sinister grin of his, Tobey told her he wanted to "kick it all up a notch."

Tobey and I were always in sync on every decision about the game, but when I heard him say that I got a bit worried. Molly had no idea what he even meant, but I sure as hell did: Tobey wanted the blinds to go up to $200 and $400, no limit, with a minimum buy-in of fifty thousand dollars. Fifty grand, just to sit and play!

Sorkin's film made it appear as if Molly tried to argue against the increase, but truth be told Tobey never asked her. He told her. Molly had absolutely no qualms about this decision for the simple fact that she didn't make any financial decisions for the game whatsoever. Nor did she guarantee the game, and she sure as hell never set the house rules, no matter what's implied in the movie. Up to this point, Molly had never guaranteed a seat . . . she never had that power—every player was approved or vetoed by Tobey period, end of story. Thankfully for me, Tobey always took my opinions into consideration and would consult with me on pretty much every decision made on behalf of the game.

"Molly's game?" Don't make me laugh. It was our game.

Think of it like this: if this were an episode of Aaron Sorkin's hit show *The West Wing*, Tobey would be the president, I was his chief of staff and Molly was our press secretary.

Only this wasn't an Aaron Sorkin fiction: this shit was real life. And kicking it up a notch to 50 gees minimum buy-in and double the previous blinds suddenly put me in the danger zone. We had such a great little hustle going with the low $5k buy-in and $100/$200 blinds . . . my feeling was, why rock the boat?

But Tobey wanted to push it all as far as he could. He wanted to see bigger pots, take home bigger wins, and destroy bigger fish. And why the hell not, he had the bankroll to sweat that kind of risk without blinking.

I did not. Sure I was making stacks of cash out of the game, and my own business was doing very nicely thank you . . . but I was not a movie star worth north of 50 million or trust-fund kid or heir to a fucking banana fortune. I had no safety net. For me, the risk was real.

But what could I do? I knew my seat in the game was completely at Tobey's discretion, so I just went along with it even though it scared the hell out of me. Sure we were buddies, but let's not kid ourselves: the game was bigger than our friendship. Business is business, simple as that.

With the blinds starting out at $200 and $400 and the $50k buy-in, I knew there was going to be a few million spread around the table at every game. And this wouldn't be like playing in the dealer's choice games with the Armenians out in Glendale where I could completely control the outcome every time I dealt. I was simply gonna have to play great poker . . . knowing that one bad move and I could be toast.

So I did the sensible thing and hedged my bets. I decided to mitigate my risk and get some backing from guys with much deeper pockets than mine. In Sorkin's film, Player X (Tobey) tells Molly that he has been backing Harlan Eustice (who was supposed to be me) for over two years. That was another lie. Tobey and I were partners in a sense, but I never asked him to stake me. He knew we were both hustling the game, but at the same time he knew I had built my own success outside of poker, as well.

So I needed some insurance, someone to stake me. At the time I was in postproduction on *The Ultimate Blackjack Tour*, which was going to air on CBS. It was a big show with a huge online gaming component to it. Imagine the thrill of blackjack combined with the skill of poker. It was being talked about by all the big poker pros, and it brought a lot of blackjack experts out of the shadows. And the man behind it all was 1994 World Series of Poker champion Russ Hamilton.

Out of all the hustlers I've ever known, none even came close to Russ. Whether it's poker, golf, or a gum-spitting contest, you never want to make a wager with Russ unless you're ready to lose a ton of dough. He might even lose a bet to you on purpose just so he can beat you for more money down the road at something else.

Remember my friend Kasey Thompson? The guy Tobey let off the hook for a million bucks out of the kindness of his heart? Well, one time Kasey had a million-dollar golf game set up with Russ. He was confident he would win because he had a much better handicap than Russ did. The day before the game, the two of them were having lunch near a big old palm tree. Out of the blue Russ bets Kasey ten grand that he can't shimmy up to the top of the tree in under five minutes. Kasey not only took the bet, but he shot up the tree like a monkey and then came back down to collect his winnings—which Russ quickly paid, in cash.

And what happens the next day out on the first fairway? Kasey's hands were so scarred up and mangled from climbing the tree that he could barely hold his driver and his golf game completely went to shit.

Unlucky coincidence? Or as sweet a long-range scam as you'll ever find? You decide . . . but suffice to say Russ easily took Kasey for the million bucks on the golf course that day. And unlike Spider-Man, he made him pay.

Before becoming a world champion poker player, Russ led an elite blackjack team and was well known as a dangerous card counter in the blackjack circles. I once saw him bet a guy that he would get kicked out of any casino for playing blackjack in less than 20 minutes. They bet ten grand . . . and Russ sat down at a blackjack table. After half an hour Russ was asked to quit playing. He lost the bet by ten minutes but made $25k while at the table, so he still came out on top! Now that is what you call a "sharp" gambler.

Russ was an old-school hustler and had an edge on just about everything. He was also the guy who started online poker giant Ultimate Bet, which at the time was still one of the biggest online poker sites around. And now, *The Ultimate Blackjack Tour* was joining the Ultimate Bet family, and I was the executive producer of the TV show and the marketing and strategic consultant for the entire enterprise. Russ and I had been working closely together, and he had of course heard about the big poker game I played in.

If I was going to get anyone to stake me, I figured he'd be the man for the job.

When I asked him about it, Russ told me that if I got him invited to the game, he would stake me for sure. I knew that getting a stone-cold pro like Russ on board wasn't gonna fly with Tobey, but I gave it a shot. And so Tobey cut a deal: Russ could play if he gave up some kind of edge. That is when Russ offered to play without ever looking at his cards!

Russ was no dummy: he figured that if he could entertain Tobey for an hour with his advanced gambling prowess, Tobey would unlock the restraints and let Russ play the game without any handicap.

What I saw next was nothing less than a master class in the art of hustling. Russ managed to actually win most of the pots he was in without ever looking at his cards. It was truly beautiful to witness. After an hour had gone by, he was still close to even. He had been making fifty-thousand-dollar raises just by reading his opponents' faces and getting them to fold and run scared . . . and all this despite them knowing he hadn't even seen his hole cards! (Or had he?) This is the same guy who could memorize the order of an entire deck of cards off one glance. All Russ needed was a seat at the table that gave him the ability to glimpse his own cards as they were being tossed to him, and he could pretend to play totally blind. Even catching one out of two cards would give him tons of information to bet with.

Even still, after about an hour he asked Tobey to let him look at his cards and continue playing normally. Tobey was having none of it. He had made a deal and he wasn't backing out of it: if Russ wanted to stay in the game, he had to continue playing blind for the rest of the night. Russ shrugged, shook Tobey's hand, and then said good-bye to everyone at the table and I walked him out.

As we left he laughed at what a ballbuster Tobey was . . . and then he turned to me and said, "Consider yourself staked . . . any limit you want, Houston, just let me know how you do after every game."

Boom . . . my worries were over. I would give Russ 50 percent of my wins, but he would cover 100 percent of my losses. This allowed me to play without sweating the fact that everyone at the table was in for about half a million each and every time we played.

What happens when you make the perfect deal for yourself? Apparently if your name is Houston Curtis you find a way to talk yourself out of it. Aside from one loss that Russ covered, I ended up going a month straight booking nothing but wins. I was doing so well, I told Russ I was gonna go it alone—every time we played I was winning over $100k. But instead of being happy about winning with no risk whatsoever, I was just pissed that I had to pay Russ 50 percent of my wins for insurance that I wasn't using. Call me greedy if you like, but I was on a hell of a roll, and I wanted to maximize the profit while I could. That's the American way, right baby?

It got so ridiculous that Tobey and I started making twenty-five-thousand-dollar side bets just to see who could go the most games without a single loss. The first time we did it, I got nine out of ten and Tobey had eight. The second time, we tied on nine winning sessions in a row. On that particular run, I remember winning over three million dollars without incurring a single loss.

At this level, with these stakes, the kind of wins I'm talking about were basically unprecedented. Hell, we were making more money than 99 percent of the professional poker players around the globe. The only thing we had to worry about was stocking the pond with fat enough fish for us to feast on every week. And, say what you like about her, that's where Molly Bloom stepped up to the plate.

All it took was a little job security pressure from Spidey, and Molly cranked it into 5th gear. One of the first players to attend the "big game 2.0" was a guy named Dave Garden. At the time, all anyone knew about Dave was that he was a known Las Vegas whale in his early thirties and was somehow involved in the circuit-breaker business. Aside from being filthy rich, Dave came off as a regular guy. He was a supernice, genuine dude, a boy scout really. This guy had more money than anyone in the room and he was a friggin' volunteer police officer once a week in West Hollywood. Why? Hell, I didn't bother to ask.

Then there was Guy Laliberté, the creator of Cirque du Soleil! Guy was making about 300 million a year from his shows and had just sold 20 percent of his company for a cool billion dollars! Oh yeah . . . and he was a degenerate gambler who was just learning how to play poker at the time! I still crack up when I look at his Wikipedia page and it actually lists "poker player" as one of the things he does professionally. So as the game shifted from The Viper Room to secluded suites and chalets at Hollywood's most exclusive hotels and the stakes soared accordingly, the personnel shifted, too. At this point, in addition to Tobey and me, our regulars became Ben Affleck, Larry Haun a.k.a. "Old Spice," Bad Brad, Dave "Big Game" Garden, commercial real estate mogul Bobby "eight/five off suit" Safai (because he liked to crack over pairs with that particular shitty hand), hedge fund operator Mike "Deep Stack" Baxter, The Hangover director Todd Phillips, and a very dapper cat by the name of Bosko, whose last name was impossible to pronounce. Tobey and I had poached Bosko from Gabe Kaplan's old timers pot-limit game. Gabe was once the it man of the so-called celebrity poker world. That world belonged to Tobey now, and he had no plans of giving it back anytime soon.

All I knew about Bosko was that he was always wearing a $10,000 suit and was rumored to be married to a ninety-year-old billionheiress. Apparently back in the day Bosko was quite the ladies' man. Plus, Doyle Brunson once shared with us that Bosko used to be a legit poker rounder back in the old days! Even though he would often go off the rails, he was a scary and fearless player, to say the least.

In addition to these we had our "semiregulars" who included Rick Salomon (whenever he wasn't chasing tail or in rehab), *The Notebook* director Nick Cassavetes, hedge fund mogul Jon Brooks and producer/club owner and high-stakes gambler Chuck Pacheco. The other, smaller fish were starting to get swallowed up by the sharks, which is what made players like Larry Haun and Brad Ruderman so important. Every week we'd fleece them . . . and every week they'd come back for more. It seemed perfect.

As for me . . . I was living the American Dream! I felt like I had completely conquered the world: my business was booming; my beautiful wife, Bonnie, had just had our first darling daughter, Chloe; and at any time I could have paid off the entire mortgage on my first home, which I had bought for $700k—hell, a couple of good nights at the table and I could have paid it off in cash.

But instead, I said fuck it, onward, upward, let it ride, speculate to accumulate . . . and so instead of paying off the mortgage, we sold the house for a little over a million bucks and handed over three times that for our 5,500-square-foot dream home. It had a swimming pool, jacuzzi, guest villa and outdoor basketball court, and after moving in, the first thing I did was install a world-class entertainment system featuring nine giant flat screen TVs with everything connected through Kaleidoscope, which was like a predecessor to Apple TV that allowed you to access a shit ton of movies from anywhere in the house. To top it off, everything was in 7.1 Dolby Surround sound. This is back when plasma screens cost about seven grand a pop and I had them everywhere. I even had a flat screen in the bathroom.

For the first time in my life it felt like money was no object. So while I was throwing checks around like confetti, I purchased a formal dining room table that was hand carved and imported from Italy for twenty-five grand, got myself another Mercedes (I had the CL65 AMG and the S63 AMG) and bought my wife a big Mercedes SUV for her and little Chloe.

And I didn't stop there. I bought my mother her dream home along with a Lincoln, bought my dad a music store to run in his retirement, and bought my brother Jimmy, who had recently gotten divorced, a new house, as well. Hell, I even bought my old karate instructor Tim Prodyma a building for his dojo back in Illinois where I grew up. Why? Because I had promised him that if I ever became a millionaire I would buy him a dojo. So . . . I kept my promise.

I even had an exit strategy. I set a goal for myself: once I had $25 million net in cash, I would walk away from poker and stop hustling forever.

I truly felt like I had life by the balls. All I needed to do was keep winning. And at that time, winning was easy.

It's difficult to describe just how it felt coming home from a game after a big win. Bonnie and Chloe would be asleep, and I would walk out into my spacious backyard and stare up at the stars above LA. It might sound like sacrilege considering how I earned my money, but while I was standing outside looking into the night sky, I would thank God for blessing me with such a wonderful life.

I had come to this town with absolutely nothing. Not a pot to piss in, no family connections, no rich uncle to set me up with a home or career . . . nothing. And there I was, about to turn 35 years old and a self-made motherfucking millionaire. God bless America.

Away from the game things were going great for me. I owned a major stake in a new online gaming website and had two TV series on the air, *The Ultimate Blackjack Tour* on CBS and *Wrestling Society X* on MTV. I was also producing pilots for three other networks, and my company, Big Vision Entertainment, had become one of the top-selling special interest direct-to-video distributors in America. And if that weren't enough I was part-owner of the hottest night club in LA at the time called Villa, which is where a lot of buddies from the game hung out, including Leonardo DiCaprio.

And best of all, I was making millions of dollars playing in the biggest poker game in Hollywood history.

I never had less than three hundred grand in cash stuffed in my private safe at home. I'd walk around with twenty grand in my pockets like it was spare change. Two, sometimes three nights a week, you would find me in the penthouse suite of a five-star hotel in Beverly Hills sitting with the Hollywood elite, playing the game I loved while getting my shoulders rubbed by a professional masseuse and eating catered food from LA's most exclusive restaurants.

Things couldn't have been better. I'd cut loose from Russ, so I got to keep everything I won, and Tobey and I—with a little help from Miss Bloom—had found a group of guys to play against who would not only never run out of money, but also never become good enough poker players to beat us in the long run. I was on top of the world. What could possibly go wrong?

CHAPTER 7

HOOKERS, COCAINE, SUNKEN TREASURE, AND BRAD RUDERMAN

I don't claim to be a genius poker player, but I've certainly been around—and in that time I've learned a few things. One of them is that the single most important factor when it comes to winning in high-stakes poker is not to be found in any book or instructional video or even by studying the pros: It's not how you play, but when you play, where you play, and most importantly, who you play with. Winning big has more to do with picking your game than just about anything else.

Sure, I could sit down and try to take pots off the best players in the world. And over the years I've done just that. You can't become good at something, anything, without surrounding yourself with those who are better than you. But the really smart player only uses those experiences to learn and grow and perfect his or her own play. When it comes time to make a living, game selection is everything.

Tobey and I had engineered such a beautiful scenario that sometimes I couldn't believe my good fortune. Don't get me wrong: doing what we did took a whole lot of cojones—it takes a certain kind of person to sit down with big money on the table and have the stomach to fire off a $100k stone-cold bluff, just because that's what needs to be done in order to win the pot. I had it right then, sure enough . . . but let's just say my gut would soon be put to the test as our game grew bigger and badder.

One of the guys who was playing around that time was a young record label owner named Cody Leibel. He was also the heir to a Canadian construction fortune and the older brother of Blake Leibel, the infamous trust fund graphic novelist who has since been convicted of killing his model girlfriend by scalping her and draining her blood. He's serving life without parole.

The first game I played that involved Cody was also typical of some of the shit that was beginning to go down about then. As soon as I walked into the suite at the Four Seasons that night, I saw him talking to Molly.

"Did you get them a room, too?" he asked her. And Molly replied with kind of a whisper: "Don't worry, you're all set."

Cody was a sweet but eccentric guy. He had these bugged-out eyes, and every time you raised him or bet into him he would nervously say, "Are you serious?"

Still, he handled defeat like a champ. I had already busted him for about $50k in the first half hour of the game that night, and he was all smiles. Then all of a sudden he got up and said, "Nice hand, I'll be back in a minute," and sauntered out of the suite.

He was gone for 30 minutes. The game was short that night, which rarely ever happened, so Tobey, me, and Bob Safi basically just sat there waiting for Cody to return. We asked Molly where the hell he went, and she dodged our questions.

When Cody came back in, he was amped, strutting like a rooster and with his eyes even more bugged than usual. Before anyone could even ask him where he had been he blurted out,

"I've been banging two whores in the other room while snorting blow off their tits!"

Apparently Molly had arranged another suite and got him some hookers and a ton of blow. We all just laughed it off—I think Bob even gave him a high-five—and then we continued to play as if it were no big deal.

Whatever other fun he had, Cody also lost six figures that night. He was definitely what Tobey and I liked to call "good for the game."

And he wasn't the only one who took advantage of Molly's "whatever you want, you get" style of hostessing. On another night Darin Feinstein showed up—he and Molly had made up and he liked to drop in and liven things up every now and then. He also liked the side action . . . and on this occasion he brought two hookers with him. Not only that—they were actual twins! You could almost hear everyone's jaws drop.

He was banging them in the bedroom of our suite while we were playing and then, cool as you like, walked out of the bedroom wearing one of the Four Seasons robes. Mostly everyone else thought it was hilarious . . . but I wasn't so sure. And Tobey hated shit like that. He didn't want any controversy around the game, and, after all, we were supposed to be there to make money.

The partying could be fun, but the game was about getting rich, first and foremost. Which brings us back to exactly who we let play.

Tobey and I were damn sure we didn't want to see any of those pro players who were so desperate to get in on the action swoop in under some bogus pretense, hit us for six figures, and then never be seen again. Not on our watch! That's why, regardless of those there for the sex and drugs and good times, the players were for the most part high-profile cats who we either knew we could beat or who we knew would draw in other, fatter fish.

There were the music artists like Nelly and DJ AM who made some healthy deposits to the Tobey and Houston fund, and the occasional actor or sports figure who would come by and get felted . . . but most of our victims were more interesting than just your everyday run-of-the-mill celebrity.

Case in point: Dwight Manley.

Manley not only negotiated contracts for some of the biggest athletes in the world, including Dennis Rodman and Karl Malone, but get this: he'd made his fortune from finding a massive sunken treasure!

According to *Forbes*, the Gold Rush-era loot he pulled from the Atlantic Ocean is the largest treasure unearthed in American history—and even became the subject of a book, the 1998 bestseller *Ship of Gold in the Deep Blue Sea*. Seriously, you couldn't make this shit up, right?

But while Manley might have been a good sports agent and an even better treasure hunter, he wasn't much of a poker player. He was typical of those who passed through the game at that time: he would stop by, become enamored with the celebs for a few weeks, lose a few hundred grand, and then move on.

Which was great, of course, but what we really sought out were the guys who could not only keep losing week after week, but would still happily return to do it all again—either because they were a stupidly rich degenerate gambler, or a stupidly rich celeb-worshipping social climber.

And one day we found the perfect whale, a man who combined both those criteria: one Brad Ruderman.

I'm pretty sure she doesn't mention it in her book, but a lot of the credit for grooming Ruderman in the first place—and then keeping him coming back for more punishment—has to go to Molly Bloom. Give the girl credit; when it came to Ruderman, she laid it on thick. She set him up on dates with her girlfriends, listened to his love problems—hell, Molly even joked with me about the time she attended his mother's funeral! The guy was basically a social idiot who had absolutely no clue how to talk to anyone, let alone a woman . . . and as for the kinds of girls he was seeing hanging out with our crowd, forget about it.

So what does Molly do? She hooks the poor sap by setting him up on dates with some of her hottest gold-digger girlfriends. Hell, I think some of them were even high-priced call girls. Of course, Ruderman was so damn weird and creepy that after one date they would tell Molly, "No way am I doing that again." But by then it wouldn't matter—there was always another girl willing to earn a few bucks in hopes that a date with Ruderman might get her invited to serve drinks at the game or even lead her to a party with DiCaprio, Affleck, or Spidey.

Despite Ruderman seemingly having more than just a few screws loose, what's truly shocking to me is that this idiot was able to swindle so many people into investing into his bogus hedge fund. We had other big hedge fund players in the game, and none of them were anything like Brad. There was Mike Baxter, who was a quiet guy but had a lot of gamble in him . . . and apparently even got banned from casinos years ago for counting cards at blackjack. You may recognize Mike's name from the *Late Night Poker* TV show.

Then there was Jon Brooks. He was a major pain in the ass to play with—always bragging about how he got such a good deal buying Brad Pitt and Jennifer Aniston's house in Beverly Hills after they split up—plus he was a supercheap tipper to the massage girls, Molly, and the dealers. But it was also obvious why he had a successful hedge fund. He was methodical, took few risks, knew when to bet big, and never gave away anything he didn't have to.

But Ruderman . . . he was a different story. Every week someone would ask these guys questions about how their fund was doing, and according to both Brooks and Baxter it always seemed there were ups and downs, peaks and troughs, feasts and famines. But not Ruderman. Every time we asked Bad Brad about his fund, he would immediately tell us how he was up again for the month and it was all going great. After a bit of this we just figured he was some kind of idiot savant. Billionaire Alec Gores told me he had invested 10 million with him, so he had to know his shit, right?

Well, it turns out we got it half right. He was no idiot savant . . . he was just an idiot, who by some miracle had managed to lie well enough to his wealthy family and close friends to get their money. He was a mini-Madoff in the making and we didn't even know it.

But, of course, at the time, I didn't give a damn where his money was coming from. All I cared about was the fact he was writing me a six-figure check almost every week.

Here's how bad at cards Bad Brad really was. One time he got in a huge hand with Rick Salomon, and Rick, being the wild man he is, made a monster all-in bluff with absolute air. He literally had jack high. Ruderman thought about it for a couple seconds, then, with all the confidence in the world, said, "I call!"

Salomon laughed, said, "You got me," and turned over his jack high. Then Ruderman turned over his hand . . . which was also jack high for a chop (which means they would split the pot). What the hell? You've either got to have a read on somebody like Daniel Negreanu only dreams about or else be the biggest moron who ever played cards to make a call like that.

Tobey and I looked at each other in disbelief. Everyone sat there scratching their heads for what must have been at least five minutes before I came to the inescapable conclusion that Brad simply had no idea how to play poker. I'm not saying this hyperbolically; I mean, he didn't even know the rank of hands. He didn't know what a straight was, or what a flush was. It was insane to see someone losing this kind of money who couldn't even grasp the most rudimentary fundamentals of the game. Hell, he might have thought he was playing blackjack for all I know. It got to the point where I even felt a kind of moral uneasiness with his stupidity.

In Molly's movie, Jessica Chastain pulls Brad aside and offers to get him a professional poker tutor . . . which, like so much else in that film, was complete horseshit. It was Tobey and I who made that offer. We bought him a bunch of books, and I gave him the poker instructional DVDs I had produced with Phil Hellmuth and Annie Duke. I figured that even if the finer tactical points were beyond him, he could at least learn the rank of hands, for Christ's sake.

But Brad didn't seem interested in learning not to lose. Instead he just came back week after week dumping an alarming amount of money to us. He had to be the biggest donkey in the history of donkeys. I started calling him "Megamillions" because every time I saw him it was like hitting the fucking lottery.

Things were about as crazy as they could get . . . and then they got crazier. And the catalyst wasn't Bad Brad, but another prize bullshitter.

Jamie Gold was a once-upon-a-time Hollywood manager who had just won the largest poker tournament payday in history. Twelve million dollars at the World Series of Poker—the biggest win then and, as of the writing of this book, one that remains the biggest WSOP win of all time. I had met Jamie before . . . and a guy I worked with, Sam Korkis, knew him very well. Sam told me from the beginning that Jamie was not a pro but enjoyed playing poker and was a lucky bastard who ran into a pile of Christmas.

Sorkin's film made it seem as if Molly tried to talk Tobey into bringing Jamie to the game based on her uncanny research. Again, complete and total horseshit. Tobey and I targeted Jamie out of the gate. He was perfect because he not only suddenly had a whole heap of lucky cash, but his entertainment industry ambitions meant he had a huge hard-on for hanging out with celebrities and acting like a big shot.

What really cracked me up was sitting there watching Jamie talk to guys like Alec Gores, Bob Safi, or Todd Phillips about living in Malibu. Jamie made it sound like he owned this big mansion there, but I knew for a fact that he had a rented studio apartment just shy of the Malibu border. He truly was and is a bullshit artist extraordinaire.

One week he came to the game showing off his new Patek Philippe watch. Being a watch lover, I naturally asked to see it— and as soon as I set eyes on it I knew it was fake. Not only was the design and weight off, but it didn't even have Swiss movement. It was a cheap quartz clicker knock-off, the kind you get down at Venice Beach or from a New York street hustler. When I pointed out to him that it was a fake, he immediately said it was a gift. The next week he showed up with a new watch and was eager to show it to me. I was thinking it would be a Rolex or Breitling . . . because

I told him he needed something with Swiss movement. Well . . . you ever see those cheap, so-called Swiss watches they sell in the *Sky* magazines on airplanes? That's exactly what he had bought.

This guy was too much. He would order thousand-dollar bottles of wine for dinner when we played, which made us all roll our eyes. I mean, sure, why not and all, but for Christ's sake, even guys like Alec, who probably has the best wine cellar in Beverly Hills, wouldn't have the stones to just toss a thousand-dollar bottle of wine on the tab . . . a tab which, naturally, came out of Molly's tips. That didn't show class. It showed the opposite, in fact; it showed just how cheap he really was.

You couldn't tell him that, of course. Jamie felt that he had earned his celebrity status and he was gonna live it up. And unfortunately, the more he tried to fit in with this crowd, the more he stood out like a whore in church. He spun tall tales that were so ridiculous it was all I could do to not burst out laughing. For instance, one time a group of us were with him on a private jet trip to Vegas, and I overheard him telling a story about how he was actually worth over 100 million dollars before ever winning the WSOP . . . but he was a victim of identity theft and got cleaned out. What??? Unreal. Another whopper had him telling us how he placed a $100,000 bet on a single number at the roulette table immediately after he won the main event. For the record: getting a casino to take that kind of action on an inside single number bet is completely unheard of. It simply couldn't happen . . . not even with balls as big as Benny Binion himself.

But for all Jamie's bullshit, it was his joining the game that amped it up beyond anything to that point. The aggressive way that he played grew our already huge game like never before. The first night Jamie joined us I won over 250,000 dollars. The second time he played, I won over three hundred grand. And that crazy hand I talked about in the prologue . . . that night I won nearly $500k!

But if I was winning that big, that means others were losing big, as well. The game had gone wild—and was threatening to go off the rails altogether.

Soon after Jamie began playing, people started feeling the sting. One night Mike Baxter (who never raised his voice even when he had a big loss) got pretty steamed when he lost $750k in a single session. I was on the receiving end of about half that, and Mike asked for a few days to move some money around in order to pay. That was the first sign that got me a little worried. When a guy like Mike Baxter ends up slow-paying, you know the game's getting out of control.

A few of our sheep had finally been skinned. Ruderman was losing anything between 100 to 300 grand every single time he played and, by my calculations, was down at least a clear four million to us . . . and we just weren't sure how deep that well was gonna keep going. Brad and I both had the same bank, so whenever I would go to deposit his gigantic checks, the girls there would let me know if he had transferred the money yet. It got to where one of them would just call me every week and tell me when it was safe to make the deposit.

I'm pretty sure Larry Haun's hot young wife had left him because he started showing up less, and for all his aggression, Jamie himself had quickly dumped a good two million out of his fortune to us. The mood was beginning to change.

Worse, it seemed they were onto the hustle.

Guys like Bob Safi and Bosko had caught on to what Tobey and I were up to . . . and they began playing for blood. Bobby especially became like my archnemesis. The guy would run me down any chance he could just for sport.

I remember having a conversation around this time with Andy Bellin, who was now out of the game and living in New York. Andy always knew what Tobey and I were up to. He understood the game was designed as a hustle and advised me to make the occasional dump, just to keep things sweet.

Ugh. There is nothing I hate worse than losing . . . but the thought of losing on the square in a game where the money isn't secretly going to an ally just made me ill. The only guy I ever met who hated losing as badly as I do was Tobey.

But unlike Tobey, if I didn't show the occasional loss, it would become damn near impossible for him to justify keeping me in the game.

So what I tried to do was just gamble more in select hands with certain guys who wanted to crush me. That was perfect for Bob Safi, who ran like God had angels watching over him when he was up against me. Almost 50 percent of the time that I got involved with Bobby while holding pocket aces, I would some-how get it all-in with the best of it and then lose. He held over me like nothing I've ever seen. Not only that, but he enjoyed busting my balls about it, as well.

And nobody got more pleasure from watching my pain than Tobey. Why? For starters, he knew he had a much better chance of getting my money from Bobby than taking it from me. Plus, he knew I needed to take one on the nose every now and then, and it always provided him with a healthy dose of schadenfreude.

Then again, to be fair, on the rare occasions that Tobey got the worst of it, I would enjoy busting his chops about it, as well. That's what pals do, right?

Meanwhile, as things got darker for us and the game started feeling more like a bloody bare-knuckle fistfight than a bunch of guys enjoying themselves every week, Molly Bloom was having the time of her life. I showed up to the game early one week and saw our hostess pulling in to the Four Seasons driving a brand-new fucking Bentley! Really? A Bentley?

The girl had become the only poker hostess in the world who pulls up to the game in a damn Bentley and hits the five-star spa for a full body massage, mani-pedi, and fucking mud bath before throwing on her latest bottle service club dress and going to work running chips, slinging drinks, and ordering dinner.

Personally, it didn't bother me that much, believe it or not. I'm a live-and-let-live kinda guy. But I knew it bugged the hell out of Tobey. In her book, Molly makes Tobey out to be some kind of monster . . . mostly, it seems, because in her eyes he's a bad tipper. Here's a fact: The worst tip I ever saw Tobey give Molly was a thousand dollars.

What world do you have to live in where tipping a thousand bucks a night minimum will get you completely trashed in someone's memoirs?

And yes, it's true that Tobey did ask her to bark like a seal one night in order to get her tip, and sure, he might have crossed a line there, but then again . . . there were guys losing so much money that they couldn't keep playing. Jamie Gold had dropped two million bucks in a matter of weeks, Ruderman double that. Meanwhile, she was taking over thirty grand a night out of the game totally risk-free. It had become completely absurd and Tobey finally put his foot down.

He applied more pressure to Molly to keep finding bigger fish to fry, otherwise he was going to start capping her tips.

Instead of simply agreeing to a cap and being grateful to keep her job, Molly called me in tears over the ordeal. She knew Tobey and I were close, and I figure she thought I would put in a good word for her. And to be honest, I did.

But Tobey didn't even know the full story. I was getting some secret intel from someone else who was very close to Molly and found out that she had started doing things behind our backs that we didn't authorize. For instance, she told all of the massage girls they had to split their tips with her. That seemed pretty low to me: there she was, taking the moral high ground over the idea that we might start capping her tips, yet she was making the massage girls give up a huge chunk of theirs behind our backs!

And that wasn't all. Molly had started dipping into Manny's take. Manny was the dealer: he brought the table, the chips, set up the Shuffle Master every week, and hired relief dealers, as well. Manny and Molly were partners as far as I was concerned. I tipped them both equally every time. So when he told me that Molly was taking a bigger portion of his tips, I was shocked—and I knew that if Tobey found out, there would be hell to pay.

Molly had undoubtedly done some good things for the overall sustenance of the game, but it became clear that the whole thing was going to her head. And if she had started this adventure entranced by the celebrities, and then seduced by the money, she had quickly graduated to the dark stuff.

Setting up Bad Brad on dates with gold diggers and staying so close to him that she ended up attending his mother's funeral was one thing; sorting out Cody Leibel with an adjoining suite and a couple of coked-up whores was another . . . but it seemed there was a whole bunch of other stuff going on that Tobey knew nothing about.

Molly was becoming greedy and careless, and some of her choices were about to backfire on her in a big way.

The first time I really grasped just how much that nervous girl with the terrible poker playlist on her iPod had changed into the worst kind of LA party girl came one night after the game had ended early and I told Molly I would lock the door on my way out, as I had some emails I needed to send. I ended up crashing out in the suite only to be woken a few hours later by an unholy racket coming from the dining room area.

There I found Molly, Rick Salomon, and a whole afterparty of cocaine-sniffing, mostly naked club girls. Molly appeared to be coked out of her mind.

I said to Rick: "What the hell is going on?" and he replied, "I just came back to fuck one of these bitches."

At that point, some girl I had never seen before (and neither had he, apparently) flat out asked him if she could snort a line of coke off his cock and then blow him.

A few minutes later, after some mindless chitchat with an actress who wanted to show me how she could tie a knot with a cherry stem (clue: she wasn't about to do it with her hands), I went to use the bathroom, and that's where I saw what I assume was Molly's Louis Vuitton bag sprawled out by the sink. Next to it was a small makeup mirror lined with cocaine along with a giant bag of pain pills. I recognized the pain pills specifically because I had taken them due to a spine surgery.

When I walked out of the bathroom, Molly seemed so fucked up I don't even think she realized I was still there. The entire scene was just dark and too damn Hollywood for my taste. I slipped out unnoticed and made my way home.

The next day I was torn on whether or not I should tell Tobey about what I witnessed. On the one hand, everyone's entitled to their own private life, and, hell, if you want to hang out with hookers and party girls and snort coke and pop pills with the dude who boned Paris Hilton, good luck to you, whatever gets you through the night, right? But on the other hand, it was one thing for someone like Salomon to behave like that . . . and it was another entirely for our poker hostess to show this kind of bad behavior after hours in the suite where our game is played.

There's a saying in journalism: never become the story. Well, it seemed Molly was fast becoming the story—and the last thing our game needed was to get a reputation as a front for a bunch of after-hours parties with club girls doing blow and turning the place into some kind of porn den. Sure the game was decadent and some of the guys involved were stone-cold crazy party animals . . . but many of the others had serious reputations to protect. And, no matter what they say, all publicity is not always good publicity.

Tobey was fiercely private about the game, and he despised rumors and gossip. But on the other hand, I knew just how ballistic he would go if he knew what Molly was up to . . . and I guess I still felt kind of protective of her.

I decided to leave it alone and not say a word about it to Tobey. But I also knew Molly was heading in a bad direction . . . and all the sex and drugs and rock 'n' roll in the world was nothing compared to what I would discover next.

CHAPTER 8

MO MONEY, MO PROBLEMS

The beautiful arrogance of youth . . . and the ugly arrogance of greed

The immortal words of Notorious B.I.G. would start meaning a lot to me near the end of 2007. Until this point it had been all about the money, and raking in the cash every week had been nothing less than a blast . . . but things were beginning to get a little more complicated.

What had started as fun had become a burden. The game had me all-in, so to speak. And if great power brings great responsibility, so it seemed great money brought great headaches. I had the giant mortgage, a wife and two daughters to support, as well as a company with about a dozen full-time employees whose lives depended on me writing checks every week. I wasn't playing for kicks anymore, I was playing to maintain the life I'd sweated so hard to build. What had begun as a sweet hustle on the Hollywood elite had turned into a fucking grind . . . which I guess is just another way of saying what Biggie was trying to put across.

I felt like I had become one of those damn nits you would see at the Commerce Casino who were grinding out their rent money every day in cash games and showing up at tournaments swarming around the so-called professionals hoping they would get in a ring game. It seemed like I was having to push it to the limit just to keep up with the pace.

How did this happen? I was making hundreds of thousands of bucks taking apart the richest and most powerful guys in Hollywood. I was living the dream, right? This was all I ever wanted. And yet . . . the more I won, the more of a goddamn headache it all seemed to be getting.

Believe it or not, I found myself longing for the simpler days, when money was tight and every move I made was a lot more dangerous to my physical health than my pocketbook. There was one time in particular I kept reminiscing about—perhaps because it couldn't have been further from the million-dollar pots, five-star glitz, and anything-you-want-you-got glamour of our setup with Molly Bloom.

I was a young upstart living in Hollywood, and I ended up moving into a loft with my girlfriend at the time, who was a beautiful award-winning playwright named Stacia Saint Owens. Together we turned our loft into a small theater called The Pig Latin Embassy and hosted a ton of independent theater productions. I was producing *The Dating Game* for Columbia Tri-Star during the day and then coming home to see thirty or forty strangers packed in my living room staring at a stage that had my bed hidden behind the black curtain. We had a sketch comedy group called The Malcontents, which gave *Will and Grace* star Sean Hayes his start in the business, and we even put on a musical up there.

It was a fun and exciting period of my life . . . even if we were flat broke most of the time. We didn't even have a shower, so our friend Jerome (who was kinda like a poor man's MacGyver) helped us take over one of the floor's public bathrooms where he rolled in a janitor sink over the toilet. We then hung a hula hoop from the ceiling, put a shower curtain on it, and ran a hose from the sink with a shower nozzle on the other end that would hang over the hula hoop. Once you got the water temperature just right, you would climb up into the janitor sink to shower using the toilet as a drain. What a lifesaver Jerome was! Years later he would help me jerry-rig the power to my three-million-dollar house when I couldn't afford to pay the sixteen thousand dollar past due water and power bill.

Looking back, like much of my life, living in the loft was insane . . . but I was young, and everything at that point in my life was an exciting challenge. Plus, there was always something weird going on in this loft building, and every day brought a new adventure.

Our building was located right on Santa Monica Blvd between Vine and Gower, so the entire area was littered with everything from homeless crackheads to straight-up thugs and tons of street-walking transsexual prostitutes who were turning tricks right out in front of our building all night long, seven nights a week.

Hell, the third time my car got broken into they ripped out the entire under dash trying to hot-wire it and finally just gave up. They fucked up the door so bad that I had to ride to the studio lot every day to my usual parking spot between a Beamer and a Porsche . . . all while using a bungee cord to keep my damn door shut!

Revered acting coach Ivana Chubbuck had her class in a loft space right below us, and there were a couple of artists and photographers who lived there, as well. You would see everyone from famous actors wandering the halls to Hollywood homeless squatters hustling for quarters to cash out at the liquor store down the street.

I came home one night to find a bondage porno film being shot in our freight elevator. This dude was bent over a chair being slashed on the ass with a horse prod by a long-legged dominatrix. I just nodded and smiled and walked right on past.

For the most part nothing surprised me. But a decade later, even as mine and Tobey's game hit unimaginable highs, one event from that weird, magical time kept coming back to me—like a kind of lesson, or a reminder of a thrill I was in danger of losing.

One night at the loft I saw a bunch of guys rolling into the building with blackjack tables and a roulette wheel. I asked the guy who controlled the first floor what was going on, and he told me he was hosting an underground casino night and asked me to come by . . . but to keep it all on the QT. I thought to myself: wow, a real bust out joint, right here in my own building! How fucking cool was this!

And then, being the cocky young adventure-seeking card mechanic that I was, my own spider senses started tingling. Tingling? They were buzzing like a barrel load of bees . . .

Naturally I asked if they needed any help setting stuff up— mostly so I could not only look like a nice guy, but also do a little recon and get a closer peek at the operation while I was at it. The main thing I wanted to check out were the dealer shoes and the brand of cards they were using. I had first learned about illegal gambling setups like this from reading books like *Gambling Scams* by Darwin Ortiz, and later from real-life experience. Bust out joints were known to have gaffed blackjack shoes and roulette wheels allowing the house to get an even bigger edge than your run-of-the-mill casino in Vegas.

But from what I could tell, these guys were squeaky clean and very inexperienced. It took me less than five minutes talking to the kid who was in charge to figure out that his crew had only done this a few times before at private parties for a gaggle of rich teenagers who lived in Beverly Hills. This was their first foray into the dark underbelly of Hollywood.

After we loaded in all the tables I finally got a look at the cards. There were several bricks (a brick is 12 decks) ready to be used for blackjack, and to my delight, they were using regular old Aviator decks in blue and red. Aviators were on the cheap end of the playing card spectrum but were still decent cards that could be found at many convenience stores. Still, I was a bit shocked that these rich Beverly Hills wannabe hustlers couldn't have sprung for some custom cards. I told the crew I would see them later that night and looked forward to playing some blackjack. Then I walked straight out the door, jumped in my beat-up gold Buick with the bungee cord tying the door shut, and drove to the nearest 7-11 to try and score some Aviators. I ended up having to go to several stores before I finally found them.

Now it was time to go to work! The first thing I did when I got back was make sure to say hi to Gary (the guy who lived in the loft where the casino was being set up) and try to get a sense if he was just renting to these guys or if he was getting part of the take. Lucky for me, he spilled the fucking beans before I even got to ask—he told me he was in for a huge percentage of the profits but was also helping bankroll the game.

To be honest, I didn't have a lot of love for Gary. He was basically a douchebag rent-a-car manager for Hertz with jet-black spiked hair who was always sweating profusely. He wore oversize suits, drove a used Mercedes, and was always talking about how many films he had in various stages of development. If my making a few bucks came at his expense, then what the hell, fuck him.

After Gary admitted he was in for a piece of the profits, I decided to take my first big risk of the night. I asked him if the dealers would be dealing the cards to the players face up or face down. He said he didn't know. That's when I told him this horse-shit story about having an uncle who was a pit boss who once told me that blackjack games that deal the cards face up had a much higher chance of getting beat by card counters. Without hesitation, Gary said, "Oh yeah . . . well, I'm pretty sure these guys deal them face down for that very reason."

Bingo! You see, I know how to count cards but it's not a skill I ever tried to perfect. But on the other hand, I needed those cards to be dealt face down in order to implement a winning strategy that I had been practicing religiously since I was a teenager. When Gary let me know that he would be one of the dealers that night, I could have whooped for joy. Fucking brilliant! I told him to save me a seat to the far left and that I would see him around midnight.

Then I went upstairs, busted out my Aviator decks, and started cleaning out the aces. It was going to be very dark in Gary's loft, there were no cameras, no pit bosses, no professional dealers, and everyone was gonna be drinking and probably doing drugs. In theory it would be an easy clean . . . but I wasn't so dumb as to not prepare properly. And unlike a poker game, there is something a bit more sinister about switching out cards in a live blackjack game.

While I didn't really want my girlfriend to know anything about my plans, I did confide a bit in this guy on our floor who was an eccentric artist. I gave him 20 bucks to whisper in Gary's ear before the doors opened, "Hey, Houston's girlfriend asked me to ask you not to let him lose much money tonight, I guess he's a bit of a degenerate gambler."

The final seed was planted. I knew that Gary, being the scumbag he was, would allow me to bet big and reckless in the hope that I was gonna leave there a broken man and make him rich. Of course, I planned to do exactly the opposite.

Midnight rolled around and all of these Hollywood types started cruising in: my guess was, these guys got a bunch of their Beverly Hills buddies to come support the opening night of their oh-so-edgy illegal underground Hollywood casino. Pretty much my entire stash at that time amounted to a five-thousand-dollar bankroll that my girlfriend had no idea about: I grabbed it and told her I was just going to go check out the scene for a bit. She was always up late writing, so that was fine by her.

When I got there, I had to turn away for a moment to hide the big shit-eating grin that had spread across my face. It simply couldn't have been a better scenario for what I had planned. There was a DJ cranking dance tunes, a full bar going, and even some kind of multicolored disco ball hanging from the ceiling. Other than that, it was dark as hell with nothing but small lights that were made to look like candles sitting on the blackjack tables.

I made my way to Gary's table and was pleased to see that the money-hungry bastard had my spot reserved and waiting for me. There were five seats at the table and three other people already playing.

Right out of the gate I started betting two hands at once. And of course with the cards coming face down, the dim lighting, and all the noise and commotion happening, not to mention the fact that Gary barely knew what he was doing, it was very easy for me to start card switching almost immediately. I would look at one hand, palm a 10 or an ace, then look at the other hand and make a switch. Then, in the act of double-checking my first hand (which was just one card sitting snugly under my bet), I would put the changed-out card with it. Easy.

But all that was just to get me warmed up. I decided the best way to win big was to get the table to up their 100-dollar max bet to 500. So I started hounding Gary to raise the table limit and began shouting, swearing, calling for cocktails . . . the whole nine yards.

Gary didn't even consult with his partner—he just raised the table limit to 500 dollars. It's funny thinking back now: five hundred bucks was small change compared to the stakes I would end up playing with Tobey a decade later, but back then, it was a hell of a lot of dough to be putting on a single bet at an underground card room . . . especially when I'd walked in there with my last five grand in the world!

But who dares, wins, right? And besides: I was skewing the odds in my favor with every passing hand.

In the end I just dispensed with subtlety altogether. I literally had a stack of aces tucked under my knee and every time I got a 10, I would switch the second card out for one of them. They must have thought I'd hit the hottest streak of my life: I was calling blackjack after blackjack like the luckiest sonofabitch ever to walk the earth. If this were Vegas I would have been tossed within three minutes trying to pull off a routine this aggressive . . . but this wasn't Vegas, and these guys simply couldn't handle me. Plus, I figured I needed to hit them fast and hit them hard because chances were, I was never gonna see them ever again after that night.

Eventually, I got to $15,725.00 up and told Gary I needed to cash out. At this point, his partner was sweating the action too, and they both looked like they were going to be sick. The entire game stopped while Gary went to sort things out. Meanwhile, I was sweating my balls off hoping they weren't gonna be smart enough to realize the shoe had about 6 additional aces than it should have.

After about five minutes he comes back with my original buy-in plus 2000 dollars in cash rolled up in a rubber band and tells me I would have to wait until the end of the night for the rest. I knew this was complete bullshit and that if I walked out that door I was never gonna see my money. I looked around for the guy with the gun . . . these bust out joints always have a guy with a gun. And there was nobody! No security!

So I pulled off my second-best hustle of the night: taking Gary aside I told him in no uncertain terms that my best friend worked for LAPD and that if he didn't get me my money in five minutes I would have his entire operation turned upside down and his ass would be going to jail. It was a ballsy move considering I didn't know a single cop in town, nor would I ever call the police to have them raid my own building. But Gary and I didn't know each other very well, and I guess I sounded convincing because he believed me.

He pulled me into a makeshift back room that was only separated from the rest of the place by a bunch of record crates stacked about 10 feet high. His hands were shaking as he took out another five grand from his pocket. The poor bastard actually started sobbing when he handed it to me, telling me how fucked he was and how badly he had needed this night to be a success.

So what did I do? Being a good guy and not a completely heartless monster, I calmed him down and convinced him to let me deal the rest of the night until they won enough money to get me square. Unbelievably, Gary agreed to my offer immediately! I had just beaten the house, and now I was gonna be the house in order to get the rest of what they owed me!

When I went to restart the game, the players were a little surprised to see the lucky bastard who just hit a record run of blackjacks come back as their new dealer. As for me, I was over the moon they had no one running the show to check the cards and find out how many aces I had slipped in the shoe . . . and now I would be able to cover my tracks and end the night worry-free. Plus, there was one other thing about those cards that would prove to be the final icing on my proverbial cake.

Earlier that night when I was pulling the aces from my own decks, I decided to give each of them a subtle crimp that would give me the ability to do some basic shuffle tracking when the dealer went to shuffle the shoe. This ended up being even more advantageous than I had originally hoped for because now I was dealing and could use the crimps to deploy card control during my shuffle, allowing me to control all of the crimped aces.

As I completed shuffling the shoe, I announced that the table limit had now been raised to a 1,000-dollar max bet.

When hearing this, Gary nearly passed out, but I simply asked everyone to place their bets and started dealing before he had too much time to think about it. I had the aces stacked close to the top of the shoe, so I was hoping they would start betting big early . . . and they did. No one bet a grand a hand, but two guys were betting $500 and $600 a hand, and the girl was playing $200 each on two spots. And what happened? I cleaned them out, of course! Before the shoe was even halfway done, they were completely destroyed.

I ended up collecting about $6,800 from them, leaving me about a grand shy of taking home my full win. Luckily Gary's partner had collected ten grand on the roulette table and another couple grand on the second blackjack table, and I was fully reimbursed in cold, clean cash.

I tossed the cards in the trash as I danced out of there like Gene Kelly during *Singing in the Rain*. The final cherry on the icing on the cake was that as I entered the hallway to go back to my loft I saw this dude who was about 6'5" and 300 lbs just standing there like he was waiting to beat somebody's ass. Without hesitation, I grabbed a C-note and went to shake his hand. As we shook hands, I got a glimpse of the piece he had strapped underneath his vest. Like I said: there's always a guy with a gun.

Damn! Those were the days. The risks I had taken that night could have gotten me killed or seriously injured —but looking back it didn't seem like a big deal at the time: it was all part of the game. I guess that's what's great about being young, having very little responsibility, and feeling like you are going to live forever. Back then the money was small, so in my mind, the risk was, too. If I won or lost an extra couple grand at the end of a night it wasn't gonna change anyone's life.

Well, guess what. Back in Beverly Hills with Tobey . . . I was starting to feel like those days were long gone . . . and every week our multimillion-dollar poker empire was getting more and more stressful. To top it off, the girl who had placed herself at the center of it all was letting greed completely take over her weekly lotto ticket.

Not only was Molly taxing Manny the dealer and the massage girls for the lion's share of their tip money, but she was starting to take payoffs from rounders and outsiders to get them into our game. This was a major betrayal, one that I really struggled with and almost wish I didn't even know.

The first guy came in under some pretense of being the cousin of a guy we all knew named BZ. His story was: rich dude in town visiting, new to poker but a huge degenerate sports bettor. Plus, he was prepared to bring cash for his $50k minimum buy in. And since BZ was a total donkey, we figured we'd go a few rounds with him based on Molly's word.

It took about one orbit around the table for me to figure out this asshole was not who he claimed to be. Once I saw him check raise on the come, hit his hand, and then value bet the river, I knew there was no way in hell this guy was "new to poker." And I wasn't the only one . . . I saw Tobey and Todd Phillips clock his action for what it was, as well.

Then someone asked him if he had seen Dave lately. Apparently that was BZ's brother. When he wasn't able to answer questions about Dave, we made him show us his license. Turns out this fucking guy had even given us a fake name! He was from New York, so I immediately texted Andy Bellin, who confirmed it . . . he was a New York rounder. A professional. Molly had gotten so damn greedy that she decided to allow a ringer into her own game.

At this point we couldn't prove that she did it on purpose, but given everything else I knew about her behind-the-scenes greed, I was pretty goddamn certain it was a setup from the beginning. We ended up keeping the guy's buy-in money and told him to get the fuck out of the game and let everyone in New York know what happens when you try and screw us over. Later I heard that Molly had to pay him back his buy-in out of her own pocket.

Did our hostess learn a valuable lesson from that? Hell no.

A few weeks later Molly found a way to insert this young Internet pro that nobody knew (but whose face I recognized immediately). He came in on the M.O. that he was a trust fund kid with money to blow, though the truth was he had built a huge bankroll playing online poker. According to one of the poker pros I knew from the Commerce, this kid had offered Molly five grand plus 20 percent of his winnings to get him in the game. It turned out to be a bad move for him: online whiz he may have been, but he was out of his league playing with us. Tobey and I stayed late, played the kid all night long, and chopped him up till he was stuck a couple hundred grand.

But this didn't stop Molly from taking another shot. A week after that incident, Tobey was out of town, and Molly put a game together last minute out at Larry Haun's new mansion in Calabasas. Bosko and I showed up, and who should be staring across the table from us but two well-known pro poker sharps.

It was getting ridiculous. She was taking action from these guys to let them come to Larry's house and chop him up . . . and Larry was supposed to be our fish! Bosko and I stepped out five minutes into the game to try to figure out what the fuck Molly was thinking.

I also pulled Manny aside and had a talk with him to see what other shenanigans were going on. I could tell he didn't really want to rat her out . . . after all, even though she was stealing a lot of his tips, he was still making a lot of money. But I had also been noticing something else—something I was hoping Manny was gonna be straight with me about.

Thankfully he came out and told me without me having to ask. He had been raking the pot for weeks for tens of thousands of dollars. He was so damn good at it that nobody but me had noticed. Oddly enough, the only other person who said anything about it at all was Cody Leibel . . . I guess he was hyperaware of

Manny lifting chips due to all the blow he had been snorting off the hookers' tits when he went on his drug-fueled sex breaks.

Of course at the time we all told Cody he was paranoid and crazy and that we never rake our game . . . how that would be unethical, illegal, and all that shit. And we meant it, too. But now it seemed Molly was forcing Manny to rake the game in order for him to keep his job. Bob Safi already hated Manny and wanted a new dealer, so poor Manny was already hanging on by a thread and doing whatever he could to save his own ass. I think Manny knew that I knew about the rake, and he wanted to come clean before me or someone like Tobey (God forbid) called him out on it.

It put me in a horrible position. Even though I knew exactly what was going on, I always want to believe the best in people. Molly was like my sweet little sister—or she'd started out that way, at least. I felt like I had looked out for her over the years and always had her back. And now it turned out the hustler was getting hustled. Molly Bloom had become a straight-up gangster. She was willing to fuck over her friends, her lovers, her employees, and the people who made her rich . . . all because of greed.

And yet, even then, as much as it broke my heart to see what she was turning into, I didn't want to completely rat her out to Tobey for fear of the game falling apart. At this point, the swings were getting so big that the only thing guaranteed was the fact that poker is a long game . . . and as long as I stuck in it, I would always come out on top.

At least, that's how I saw it. But Tobey was already figuring things out on his own, and it wouldn't be long before he would put his foot down with Molly Bloom. And I would find out in the worst possible way that the cocky, brilliant, untouchable young hustler who cleaned out the underground casino on Santa Monica Boulevard and then turned dealer to win it all back from everyone else had got myself into a situation that was simply too big for even me to handle. Finally, fatally, I was getting out of my depth.

CHAPTER 9

JUMPING THE SHARK

By this point, the game had changed. On the one hand, it was a lot less fun. Tobey was getting more and more irritated with Molly, which, as well as souring the atmosphere, seemed to put a lot more pressure on her to go the extra mile to prove her worth, scrambling for players in order to overcome his worries and at the same time fueling her desire to be sneaky and underhanded at every turn. It all began to get a bit desperate: one night Molly brought in an ex-NBA pro from Detroit to play. This guy dumped fifty grand and then flat-out refused to pay—making him the first guy to ever stiff us in the history of the game.

Twenty-seven thousand of that fifty grand was supposed to come to me that night, so I was pretty pissed, to say the least. What made it even more ridiculous was the reason he refused to pay was that he claimed he was cheated. Obviously we all knew that was bullshit. If I remember correctly, he lost his last $20k betting all-in against Todd Phillips, who felted him. Seeing as how Todd was well on his way to being worth over 100 million due to the backend deal he made for himself when directing *The Hangover*, the idea of Todd cheating anyone was a joke.

But on the other hand, the game was still on a forward trajectory. Guys like Guy Laliberté (creator of Cirque du Soleil) had been coming along regularly, as were a string of big money players like Rick Salomon and Dave Garden, and then there was still the steady action of Larry "Old Spice" Haun and Bosko. Sure, some were definitely feeling the pain of their losses, but it hadn't gotten to the point where anyone had gone belly-up. Not yet anyway.

Another positive from that time is that I noticed we had become comfortable enough with one another that everyone started sharing more personal information about themselves, opening up a little as buddies as well as guys who played poker together. Alec Gores casually revealed how he bought this company that had undervalued itself and ended up making 900 million on the deal literally upon purchase. Alec also tossed me some distribution business from one of the clients repped by his little brother's Agency Paradigm. Brad Ruderman was of course always pimping his dirty hedge fund while dumping truckloads of money to the game, and one time even Bob Safi stepped up with a real estate investment tip, nothing illegal or "insider," but solid expert info that Tobey and I jumped on.

By 2007 our lives had changed quite drastically since this game began, and we had gone through a lot of those changes by one another's sides. Especially me and Tobey. When I first met him hustling at the Commerce, Tobey was a single guy living a pretty wild life—now he was comfortably one of Hollywood's big players, settled down, married and with a daughter. I had gone from living in a modest home to a 5,500-square-foot mansion in Sherman Oaks, driving $200,000 cars, putting my kids in private school, and flying around with celebs in private jets! It was surreal.

I remember one time I was driving Tobey home from the game and we ended up pulling over in Beverly Hills just to watch the

Me at the Commerce Casino in 2004.

Me, sixteen years later, at Kardsharp Studios.

With Tobey Maguire at his house on his thirtieth birthday.

Tobey and Jen with me and the family at my thirty-fifth birthday party.

Poker buddies (left to right): Tobey Maguire, actor David Bordolucci, Houston Curtis, producer and night club owner Chuck Pacheco.

Discussing poker strategies with Tobey.

Toasting with Tobey

"I need this shoot to end so I can get to my real job!"

In the studio with Cheech and Chong and Lou Adler

Money won from a poker game that I used as a prop on a video shoot.

On set shooting a commercial with actress Natasha Henstridge.

On the set with poker champ Phil Hellmuth.

Poker champs Phil Hellmuth and Kenna James with me at the Commerce Casino in 2004.

On set in Beverly Hills shooting Phil Hellmuth's *Million Dollar Poker System* DVD with fellow poker players from the big game: writer Andy Bellin, Phil, power broker entertainment attorney Jon Moonves, and myself.

Smiling on set. Always good to enjoy your work!

Poker instructional DVD and TV series I created and executive produced.

The video franchise I created with partner and childhood friend Rick Mahr that made me a millionaire.

With my brother Jimmy Carter, opening a burger joint after my heart attack.

My sister (Darla Moore), Jason Gordon Thomas, and me in Beverly Hills.

My family in Los Angeles (left to right): father-in-law Andrew Buckley, father Mack Curtis, daughter Chloe, and mother Norma Curtis.

The beautiful Bonnie Buckley Curtis, mother of my children.

With my wonderful daughters, Chloe and Callie Curtis, the day before I lost a million dollars in one night.

Throwback shot to 1991, with my
mother Norma Curtis.

With my best friends, Steve Pacey and Dave Weidenhoffer,
joined by our then-manager, the late Jim Patterson.

"…much deception is practiced at cards, but it is one thing to have that knowledge and quite another to obtain a perfect understanding of the methods employed, and the exact manner in which they are executed."
—S. W. Erdnase, *The Expert at the Card Table*

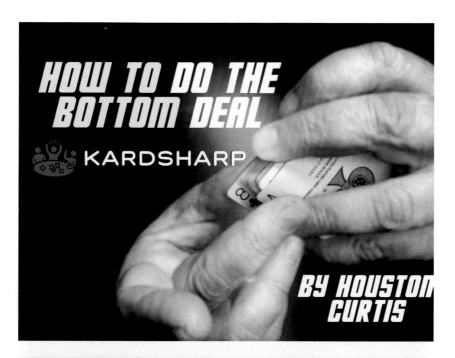

Now retired, I consult for the gaming industy and teach the dark art of card manipulation at Kardsharp.com.

Feeling like a million bucks at my favorite place: the poker table.

sun come up and shoot the shit about life and love and some of the crazy shit we'd gone through.

He shared some stories of his wild youth—which also served to explain pretty much why he had sworn off alcohol completely. (At least that was the case in those days.) He told me how he and Leo used to go through the celebrity magazines and circle all of the girls they wanted to hook up with. Not in a fantasy wish list way . . . but in a practical sense, like marking up items in a shopping catalogue. Those dudes would not only make lists, they'd put the girls in the order they wanted to, ahem, meet them, too.

He said he had a huge crush on Alyssa Milano when he was younger, so she was one of the first he had to check off his list. He told me about getting out of control at a party once and finding himself in a threesome with two huge starlets whose names I will not mention. He was attracted to one of them sure enough, but he told me the other one kind of bummed him out, so he ended up slipping out of the room and hooking up with some other TV actress who was just coming on the scene. I gave him heat for that . . . walking away from a threesome with these particular superstars . . . not something many guys would ever do.

There was a mutual respect between the two of us that extended beyond poker. I was fascinated with how he had managed his career . . . and he seemed genuinely interested in the out-of-the-box ideas I had, and how I came to LA with nothing and made something out of my life. Despite the millions in the bank, the A-list friends, the casual threesomes with Hollywood's hottest starlets, he wasn't that much different from me, deep down. He still remembered his roots. He told me about eating at soup kitchens with his mom when he was little, how they'd save and scrimp so he could go on auditions.

We attended each other's birthday parties, our wives had lunches together, our kids had begun to play together . . . I was on set with him when he shot the final scene of *Spider-Man 3* for Christ's sake. We were close, like brothers. At least that was my take on it.

While many of the game's other regulars had become crucial to my weekly income, I had also become pretty tight with some of them, as well. Guys like Bob Safi, Mike Baxter, Bosko, Nick Cassavetes, Chuck Pacheco . . . as well as Ben Affleck and Leo. It's almost impossible to sit at a table week after week with millions of dollars changing hands and not develop a few friendships with the guys sitting across from you.

It was like being part of a very exclusive club. How close were we? Let me put it this way: if a group of us had gone to Vegas for the weekend and someone needed an extra hundred grand in cash, any one of us would float it to him without question. We had a bond . . . even if that bond was based on some of us being the wolves and others being the sheep.

I figured, the closer I got with these guys, the better off my life would be. I was part of an elite crew and, I have to admit, it was intoxicating. But you know what else? It was also all just an illusion. A palace built on sand. It was a whited sepulcher: beautiful on the outside, but on the inside full of the bones of the dead. Of course, I only realized that later. And right now the whole sorry edifice was about to come crashing down around me.

Way back in 1985 a guy named Sean Connolly coined the phrase *jumping the shark*, referring to an episode of *Happy Days* where Fonzie actually jumps over a shark on water skis. *Jumping the shark* would go on to become pop culture short-hand for that tipping point where something formerly brilliant loses its magic forever. Like poor Fonzie and the *Happy Days* crew, once you've jumped the shark it's downhill all the way.

My life was about to jump the shark big time. And what a life it was.

Best of all I was married to the beautiful Bonnie Buckley, the golden girl from Holmby Hills whom my friend Andy Bellin referred to as "Beverly Hills Barbie" . . . a girl so far out of my league I still shook my head sometimes wondering how I got so lucky as to marry her.

While I grew up in a small farm and factory town in southern Illinois, Bonnie was definitely from the other side of the tracks. Her family had a home in Marblehead, Massachusetts, another in Boca Raton, Florida, two condos in West Palm Beach, and a mansion on Carolwood Drive in Holmby Hills on the same street as Michael Jackson, Walt Disney, Peter Morton, Rod Stewart, and Frank Sinatra. While I was playing in a rock band and shooting pool at the local bowling alley on my 16th birthday, Bonnie was at a debutante ball for her sweet 16 and attending Westlake School for girls with people like Tori Spelling.

Our wedding was featured by *Inside Weddings* magazine, as well as *Town & Country*; and so connected was my new family that the reception was held in the Crystal Ballroom at the Beverly Hills Hotel with over 300 guests, including business tycoons, entertainment luminaries, and actors including Jenny McCarthy, Julianna Margolis, Jennifer Coolidge, and of course Andy Buckley (David Wallace from the office), who was also my new brother-in-law and one of the groomsmen. Actor Ralph Waite gave the prayer, legendary comedian Norm Crosby gave a toast. Natasha Henstridge was one of Bonnie's 16 bridesmaids.

The one thing that kept me at least a bit grounded was the fact that my father-in-law and I were so much alike—though it didn't seem so at first. The first time I met him, we had dinner at The Ivy in Beverly Hills, and Rob Lowe came over to our table to pay his respects, saying, "Hi, Mr. Buckley. I just wanted to say hello to you and Bonnie before I left; I hope I'm not interrupting you." I was taken aback: who the hell was this guy? I dated Bonnie for a year before she would even tell me what her dad did for a living.

Turns out Mr. Buckley was one of the most successful football handicappers in gambling history and his picks had brought Las Vegas to its knees on many occasions.

From the start Bonnie swore me to secrecy, as the true identity of her father's handicapping alter ego has never been public knowledge. His true profession was hidden from everyone except for those who knew him best and had been let into the family circle. Bryant Gumbel had once asked him (under his alias) to do a regular weekly sports segment, but he refused; the guys who owned Mann's Chinese Theater asked him to put his handprints on the walk of fame because his picks had made them rich . . . but he also refused. Or, I should say his alter ego refused . . . as none of these people had ever seen his face and none knew his true identity.

Why? Well, first off, he knew his business operated in a gray area and could sometimes be a bit dangerous, hence the secret identity. But the main reason was probably due to the fact that during the height of his career, his oldest son, Fred Buckley, was playing quarterback under John Elway at Stanford . . . which could have proved slightly awkward for everyone involved. If word hit that the Stanford quarterback was the son of a famous football handicapper, it would have been bad for Fred. After

Stanford and a quick stint with the Raiders, Fred went on to create Herbal Viagra and became rich as hell in his own right.

My father-in-law's name was Andrew P. Buckley, but I just called him Mr. B—and he was a great mentor. Like me, he was every bit as comfortable sitting with Ivy Leaguers or entertainment power players as he was shaking hands with wise guys. Not only that, he had promised me that if I ever needed his help for anything, he would be there for me.

It was an insurance policy I didn't ever plan cashing in on, but like an ace up my sleeve, it was sure nice to know it was there if I needed it.

So there I am in the spring of 2008, surrounded by money, love, excitement, and glamour, supposedly living the dream . . . but despite it all, something didn't feel right. Between Molly's nonsense, the increasingly crazy stakes, and the pressures of taking care of a family, the game just wasn't as much fun anymore. And on top of it all, just like Arthur Fonzarelli strapping on his water skis in *Happy Days*, the so called "ratings" of my primetime life were about to plummet.

Hindsight's got 20/20 vision and gamblers are superstitious, so it's easy to make connections and see all kinds of portents and omens in retrospect . . . but my world collapsing, my personal shark jump, wasn't the result of a single moment. It was, to coin a phrase, an accumulation of shit. And it all began when the largest tree in Southern California came crashing down on my house.

My neighbor directly across the street was famed television writer Sol Saks. Sol had literally just turned a hundred years old. I think his wife was in her thirties, God bless him. I remember asking the realtor when I bought the house if there was going to be a problem with the tree in the front of his yard: it was the biggest damn tree I had ever seen, and it leaned way over toward my side of the street. I used to stand on my balcony and think to myself . . . if that thing ever comes down, it could kill us all.

One day I went to the car wash and left my phone behind. I couldn't have been gone more than 30 minutes, and when I returned, there were three fire trucks on my street, and sure enough, that damn tree had come down right on top of my beautiful home, taking out two of my own trees and my front gate before obliterating my second-story outside balcony and going right through the garage and master bedroom.

There were news crews pulling up, helicopters in the air, it was crazy. Bonnie, who was nine months pregnant with our second daughter, Callie, had luckily been out running errands at the time. And little Chloe, who was in the house with our nanny, was, miraculously, also unharmed. In that moment, that was all I cared about.

My brother-in-law, Brad, had actually got there before me and, unable to use the front gate, had jumped the fence in our backyard to get to Chloe and make sure she was ok. Sadly, Brad injured his back going over and still has problems today because of it. But, hero that he is, he got Chloe and her nanny Rena to safety before the fire trucks showed up. In the end it took four giant cranes nearly a month to clear the tree away from the house and off the street.

As we were effectively homeless, our insurance put us up in the Four Seasons for a month during repairs, which, if nothing else at least, made it very convenient for me when heading to the poker game . . . as it was usually just down the hall! When I told the guys what had happened, Mike Baxter (who was normally kind of quiet) cracked up so hard he got tears in his eyes.

After his laughter subsided, Mike said something I have never forgotten: "Looks like your luck is finally taking a turn for the worse, Houston."

Mike was right. Looking back, the tree was just the first sign my fortunes were about to change. Of course at the time, I just shrugged it off and told them how the insurance company was putting me up in one of LA's best hotels—not a bad silver lining, right? I figured I'd be back in the house soon, and if need be, Bonnie, Chloe, and the soon-to-be-born Callie could always go stay at her parents' house on the other side of the hill if they got tired of room service at the Four Seasons. What could I complain about?

Meanwhile, there was still the game to concentrate on: specifically, Molly's continuing (and increasingly annoying) habit of trying to weasel players into the action who were offering her money. Trust fund playboy Dan Bilzerian was one of them. In articles since, Dan likes to talk as if he were a regular in our game, but truth be told he only played once and was never invited back. Not because we thought he was too good—Tobey just didn't like the guy. I got to know Dan a bit better later on when producing a TV concept with him, and it turns out he's a pretty nice guy . . . but don't go believing he was ever a regular.

During this time, I also began to sweat a few big losses. For the most part, every time I lost upward of six figures I would win it back the following week. That being said, it was still frustrating because my bankroll wasn't growing as steadily as I would have liked, and I had been so consumed with the game that I failed to realize my non-poker-related business was about to go badly south. Hell, the entire economy from the stock market to the real estate market was heading straight for the shitter . . . and I was too busy thinking about poker to realize that the walls were starting to crumble down around me.

Remember when the online poker world came under fire between 2006 and 2007? Better yet, remember the online cheating scandal that made headlines and was cause for a special on *60 Minutes* talking about Ultimatebet.com? Well, just about the same time the construction company finished repairing my house, another bombshell went off. I woke up one morning with a call from Jon Moonves. Jon gave me a heads-up that WickedChopsPoker.com had published a huge article on their homepage with my picture under a caption that read: "IS HOUSTON CURTIS THE CHEATER BEHIND ULTIMATE BET ACCOUNT H_CURTIS???"

The worst thing that can possibly happen to a successful card mechanic is to get labeled by the poker community as a cheat. And one thing I prided myself on was the fact that throughout my entire career, whether I beat the game straight up or with the help of an ally and some card table artifice, I had never been accused of cheating (at least not in a game that mattered to my pocketbook, my life, or my reputation.) But this Ultimate Bet story had the potential to screw that up forever.

Things looked bad. Yes, I had the username of H_Curtis, but I rarely used it. It was set up by this guy named Travis who worked for Russ Hamilton. Russ was my partner on *The Ultimate Blackjack Tour,* but he was also a cofounder of the online poker giant Ultimate Bet. Apparently multiple screen names associated with Russ and Travis got called into question for using a God Mode that showed all of the players' hole cards. I could probably write an entirely different book about the Ultimate Bet Scandal, but suffice to say . . . I don't know for sure who was responsible for the online cheating, and I don't want to know!

Don't get me wrong: I knew about Russ Hamilton's reputation as a world-class gambler, card counter, and all-around advantage player, but up to this point he had always been aces in my book. And if I'm being honest, I still consider him a close friend even though a lot of my other friends in the poker world may feel differently.

It's easy to throw stones, but I've never met a pro who, given the chance to glimpse their opponents' hole cards, would "take the high road." Hell, as soon as Russ got painted as a villain, the entire Poker Ponzi scheme with rival site Full Tilt came crashing down to the tune of 430 million. Now professional poker was getting looked at with a microscope. Howard Lederer, Chris Ferguson . . . and others associated with Full Tilt got blacklisted. Even the highly respected poker pro Phil Ivey finds himself in court after being stiffed millions by two casinos for being accused of edge sorting. Ivey runs like such a god that you could probably put a smoking gun in his hand and a bucket of positively ID'd blood from a dead politician splattered all over his polo shirt and he would still manage to show up every week to play for millions at the Bellagio with all the other heavy hitters. But poker champs like Russ and Howard Lederer haven't been so lucky. Guilty or not, when rumors like this hit the Internet, someone accused of certain kinds of "advantage play" could be lucky to get invited back to the local Bingo Parlor for the weekly Father O'Malley potluck.

With help from Jon Moonves, I convinced Wicked Chops Poker to take my name down, but it was too late . . . every online poker thread had picked it up, and suddenly I was out there in a big way. Worse, I was about to close a huge investment deal for my company with millions of dollars in funding for new programming that was going to save my ass. During their due diligence, *60 Minutes* did an exposé on Russ Hamilton. Once my name got mixed up with Russ and the online cheating scandal, my investors pulled out of the deal. Instead of getting into the backstory of this deal and how important it was at the time, I'll just say this . . . it hit me harder than that damn tree that had crashed through my house months earlier.

I was soon vindicated from any wrongdoing, but the damage had been done: to my reputation and to my wallet. On top of being unfairly attached to the scandal and losing a major investment deal, the UBT would go off the air and I would get stuck for about $800k in fees and budget costs.

At the same time as things began to unravel for me, Tobey had begun really putting the screws to Molly. What started out as him casually talking about capping her tips had become a power struggle between them, and with each passing week he wanted her out more and more. He even approached me about the two of us going in on a penthouse condo and creating a private club to hold the game in. He wanted to eliminate all of the excessive tipping and hotel fees and put people on sensible salaries. And he was right! Why should a hostess be making $thirty grand a night to run a poker game when we had guys losing millions of dollars a year? Put it that way, and the whole thing was absolutely balls-out ridiculous.

Nonetheless, I convinced Tobey to hold off on making any major changes to the game and assured him (once again) that I would talk to Molly about his concerns. To be honest, I wasn't solely motivated by looking out for Molly—by this time I was getting pretty tired of her shit, too—but so much else in my life was going haywire, I figured the last thing I needed was a major restructuring of the poker game that had all but become a weekly six-figure guarantee for me.

But then like a certain dead playwright once said: When sorrows come, they come not as single spies, but in battalions. And as I was still reeling from the bad beat of losing money on the UBT, something else happened that really knocked the wind out of me. What was that thing? Two thousand and fucking eight, that's what.

The crash of 2008 hit everyone that September like a ton of bricks. Or nearly everyone. Of course, Tobey, being the lucky bastard he was, had just unloaded his three-million-dollar Hollywood Hills home to a couple of the Walton kids (that's Walton as in Walmart, not as in "G'night John Boy") for around 11 million . . . just before the economy tanked.

But me? Hell no. My luck was out every which way. I woke up one day, and my own three-million-dollar house, freshly rebuilt after having the biggest goddamn tree in Los Angeles fall on it, had suddenly plummeted in value by two-thirds. As that same dead playwright almost certainly didn't say: I was totally fucked.

So, I'm not only in the hole two million on my house, but I'd also lost a small fortune on the UBT when the online gambling law passed, rendering the show's backend profit center via advertisers and online sign-ups useless. To add insult to injury, the UBT Corporation filed an ABC (assignment for the benefit of creditors) deal and sold off the ClubUBT.com property to the World Poker Tour without consulting me. So, the shares in my online gaming empire weren't worth the paper they were printed on.

But, despite it all, I still had my production/distribution business, right? I had an overall distribution deal with First Look entertainment that could see me right. Except . . . one day my banker called and told me to be careful with these guys because they were going broke, owing me about four million dollars. Bastards! Sure enough, I had a monthly royalty check due: it should have been made out for over $500k; when it showed up the check was for forty grand. First Look? First Crook, more like.

Shit had got real. I was overextended and my business started to topple over. I had allocated monies coming into projects I had in production and development, one of which was already up and running, an independent animated film starring Cheech and Chong. I had weekly staffing fees to deal with and tons of overhead. And the money that should have been coming in to pay for it all suddenly wasn't there anymore. Between First Crook, UBT, and another distributor, I ended up getting stiffed for over four million dollars in just a few short months. That would rise to eight million in an 18-month period.

I was all out of options . . . except one. Poker was now more important than ever before. Poker was my lifeline.

But here's the thing. If poker is a game of skill (plus a certain amount of luck), it's also a game of confidence. You've got to know you're good in order to play well. And you've got to believe you're great in order to play really well. When hundreds of thousands of dollars are being won or lost on the turn of a river, when millions are changing hands every night, there's no room for hesitation, no place for fear. You've got to believe you can win, you've got to play with the certainty, the confidence that you're the best . . . because once you lose that, once you let doubt creep into your game, it's all over.

And that's where I was headed. I no longer went to the game with a desire to win . . . I sat at the table scared as hell at what might happen if I lost. Just a few weeks of running bad could cost me everything. Back in the day, Tobey and I would joke about crushing souls at the poker table—we didn't just say that stuff because we were heartless assholes. We said it to build our own confidence and winning spirit.

The winning spirit was gone—and I didn't like it one bit. Even when I was broke and struggling, back in the weird loft with my playwright artist girlfriend or hustling my way up in the smaller casinos, I'd never approached a game with a negative attitude. I was smarter than that. The old Houston would never let himself get caught up in a situation that couldn't be controlled.

But I was out of options. I needed to keep the money coming in, and it was too late to seek a backer again: the crash in 2008 had scared everyone who had liquid cash.

I got desperate: in one of my not-so-proud moments, I decided to deal with the problem by flying to Las Vegas. I still had $100k and $200k markers at just about every major casino on the strip. I figured if I could win about a half a million playing blackjack, that would increase my bankroll and allow me to float while I figured out my next move. Smart, right?

That trip to Vegas was fucking brutal. It started well enough: within a few hours I was up ninety-five thousand at the Mirage playing blackjack at five grand a hand. When I hit $95k, there was a shift change, and a new dealer came on. And, against every instinct, instead of just quitting, I was determined to cash out up an even hundred grand . . . so I made another bet.

An hour later I had given the $95k back to the Mirage and was now stuck two thousand for my full marker. So I went to Caesars and immediately dropped another $75k.

Thank Christ, I finally hit Red Rock and won $200k. After negotiating discounts from Caesars and the Mirage, I ended up only being down about $50k for the trip. Was it lucrative? No, obviously. Was it even any kind of fun? No chance: it was a fucking nail-biter . . . and sadly, would be the first of many in the coming months.

It wasn't like previous the previous trips I had to Vegas. Hell, one time I literally started out with 100 dollars screwing around on a video poker machine, and an hour and a half later I had turned that hundred bucks into $275k! However, at this point, I couldn't even access my marker at the Golden Nugget anymore because they had banned me for life due to "excessive winning" (now there's an irony), so I just flew back to LA with my tail between my legs and pretended like nothing happened.

That week at the game I played like a demon and won over three hundred thousand dollars. Finally, I felt like I was back on track. Even though my house value had bombed and my business was falling apart at the seams, at least I could still make money in the game.

I figured if I could just go on another three-million-dollar run, I would have a healthy enough bankroll to regroup and restructure my company and deal with my house. Hell, why not? I'd done it before. Plus, let's not forget, I always had my father-in-law. Remember him? Mr. B was still the ace up my sleeve.

Just so long as I could keep Tobey from firing Molly for a few more weeks and throwing off our momentum, I could literally put all my chips on the table, beat the shit out of the game, and take things from there. Easy.

I rolled up at the Four Seasons that week feeling pumped, wired, fizzing with energy. I was ready to crush souls. Not because I wanted to; not for the joy of winning . . . but because I needed to. I couldn't afford to lose.

CHAPTER 10

THE NIGHT I LOST A MILLION DOLLARS

The night my world collapsed was off-kilter from the start. Molly didn't have our usual room at the Four Seasons, and the poker table was set up on the left side of the suite instead of the right. Technically that didn't matter a damn bit, but gamblers can be very superstitious about shit like that. Was I superstitious about it? Maybe I should have been.

Molly informed me that one of the big fish who would be in attendance actually requested the room change because our regular suite hadn't been "lucky" for him. Tobey and I both chuckled—we planned to make sure this room would be even less lucky for the sucker. The others started showing up and it was time to go to work.

I hadn't planned on staying late that night because the next day was my wife's 40th birthday and I had big plans to take her out to dinner with her brothers and a group of our close friends. Plus, I had reserved a table the next day for brunch at the Polo Lounge, where she was meeting up with Tobey's wife, Jen Meyer, and some other girlfriends, as well.

About three hours into the game things were going horribly wrong for both me and Tobey. This is something that just never happened. Sure, Tobey and I would each have an occasional loss, but never together, and never this badly. But here we were: Tobey stuck for half a million bucks and I wasn't far behind him. Every river card that could hurt us was landing. It was bad beat central . . . and the rest of the guys couldn't get enough of it. I couldn't really blame them: we had been hammering them for millions of dollars over the past few years, so they were relishing in our pain. Nightclub impresario Andrew Sasson was at the game that night, and he was smiling ear to ear with glee. Bob Safi was licking his chops, as were Bosko and Baxter. And the guy who was supposed to be the big fish that night aside from Ruderman was an investment banker from San Diego who was catching cards like he was putting on a show at the Magic Castle. Even Ruderman, who had never won a game in his life, somehow managed to at least break even that night.

After midnight it was just me, Tobey, Bob Safi, and Andrew Sasson. Bobby was always good for the game, but he could be a dangerously sly player—and there was no bet too big to scare him out of a pot. Andrew was another story. On the one hand, I had been beating him for a lot of money ever since the days we were playing in Tobey's kitchen . . . but on the other, he's a smart guy and he learns fast and he had got better over the years. Tonight, he was playing well, catching cards and thoroughly enjoying himself. Also, he had just unloaded two huge condo towers in Vegas and managed to get out making millions right before the real estate crash. So . . . he was on top of the world.

Things continued in the same vein until just before 1am, when Tobey and I did something very rare for the two us. We got involved with each other in a huge pot. Tobey bet out twenty grand preflop. Bob called, Andrew folded, and I looked down at pocket jacks. I knew Tobey had been steaming and playing poorly because I had been, as well. I decided to pop it and raised another fifty grand. Tobey smooth called and Bob snap called. Fuck: this was a huge pot already.

The flop came jack, four, deuce with two diamonds. I had flopped top set and checked it to Tobey. Tobey bets seventy-five grand with Bob behind him. I figured he had to have aces, which meant that with three jacks I was about to bust my buddy. Sweet!

Bob laid down whatever garbage he was holding and now it was up to me. I knew I could milk Tobey and just smooth call him. He had to have a big pocket pair because there was no way he would have bet that much preflop without one. I figured he thought he was gonna trap me, but whichever way you looked at it, I had him crushed.

And then I hesitated. Tobey was my buddy. We weren't exactly colluding when we played, but we sure weren't trying to felt each other, either. Plus, at the end of the day, I knew it was Tobey who helped me secure a seat every week. Having said that, there was simply no way in hell I was about to soft play top set. For the uninitiated, a set is three of a kind. Since I was holding two jacks and the highest card on the flop was a jack . . . that gave me top set. So by way of reconciling my instincts as a poker player and my loyalty to my friend, I decided not to string him along—and instead went all-in. I knew that Tobey would respect an all-in bet from me and get the hell out of my way if he had anything less than a smaller set. And I knew he was definitely disciplined enough to lay down an over pair in this situation. An over pair being a pair that was higher than any card on the flop. So, in this case, aces, queens or kings.

To my surprise, a laydown never came: instead, he snap called me and immediately turned over his hand. He had ace, king of diamonds. That gave him a nut flush draw with two cards to come. He was gambling way out on the edge, and it was scary. This is the kind of move you see being made on television a lot in tournaments . . . but not in high-stakes cash games. And definitely not from disciplined players like Tobey.

But one thing I've learned about supersuccessful people—on top of getting what they want from talent and hard work, they also tend to get lucky more often than the rest of us. What was that line? The more I win, the luckier I get. It's crazy how often that's true. Tobey had been "running good" his entire life, and he wasn't about to stop now.

I seemingly had him crushed and was a huge favorite to win the hand. Even if Tobey hits his flush on the turn, I'm still live to a full house if the board pairs. It was really unlike Tobey to make a call like this. In a tournament I could understand it, but not in a high-stakes cash game with hundreds of thousands in the pot.

I asked Tobey if he wanted to run it once, twice, or three times. Running it meant that we would see the turn and river card three different times for three different outcomes, which could potentially split the pot into thirds if we ran it three times or in half if we ran it twice. In the long run it didn't change the odds, but in the short run it gave a little insurance to me against a bad beat and gave Tobey an extra chance to at least hit the flush once and get a third of the pot back. After both of us going all-in, the pot was about $400k and would help to get either one of us even for the night . . . as sick as that sounds.

Spidey may have called like a maniac, but now that the cards were turned face up he was ready to make a deal. Tobey agreed to run it three times. Manny the dealer would always make eye contact before burning and turning just in case someone changed the deal at the last minute. I gave him the nod of approval and he dealt the turn card. To my dismay it was a diamond right on the turn, and the board didn't pair on Fifth Street. One lost.

The second time we ran it, he hit a diamond on the fucking river. Tobey now had two-thirds of the pot after getting it all-in with the worst of it. Unbelievable. I watched Manny burn and turn the final time, heart hammering, bile rising. Again, the turn card was a diamond. At this point I needed the board to fucking pair; otherwise, I was going to be stuck $500k for the night.

Did it pair? Hell no. Just to add insult to injury the lucky bastard hit another diamond on the river.

Before I could even process how lucky Tobey had gotten, he let out a whoop and yelled: "Cash me out, Molly!"

I couldn't believe it. "Dude . . .," I said, "you just bad beat the living shit out of me and now you're quitting?" Tobey just flashed me that crooked smile and cracked a little uncontrollable laugh. "Sorry buddy!" he said gleefully and patted me on the back.

Producer Chuck Pacheco was in the room. He and Tobey had known each other for years. Chuck looked at me and said, "What are ya gonna do? The kid runs like God!" And Chucky was right. Tobey played well and he ran even better. Ultimately I can't blame him for wanting to leave after getting even . . . hell, I guess I would have wanted to do the same damn thing if the pot had gone my way. He didn't need to look so goddamn happy about it, though.

Tobey left, and with his departure it seemed I was fucked. And then, right on cue, like a swaggering, degenerate answer to my prayers, in strides Rick Salomon. But then, that's the thing about praying: you've got to make sure you're sending those prayers to the right guy . . . and you better be careful what you wish for, just in case you get it.

Rick was no sucker. He had more than just a big dick and a Grade A drug habit. He was a dangerous gambler, but I also knew he was my best and only shot of getting even for the night. Bob was leaving and Andrew was sitting tight on a long-overdue profit. I went to Molly and told her to give me another $500k, which would put me in the game for a million dollars. Her face dropped and I could almost feel her heart sink as I asked for it. She asked me if I was sure and reminded me about Bonnie's birthday party. I looked her right in the eye and said: "Five hundred grand or a million, what the fuck is the difference at this point?"

Reluctantly, she handed me the chips. Truth is, she didn't actually have a choice: whatever she may have thought, Molly had no authority not to extend credit to anyone in the game. The main players assumed all of the risk—all she did was set up the room, call the guys on our list, and then sit back and make a fortune off the back of it all. The only thing Molly ever risked was a few bags under her eyes from the late nights and the possibility of someone losing so bad they stiffed on her tips for the night—and that never happened. Hell, even that time she refused to bark like a seal for Tobey, he still ended up giving her a thousand bucks.

Rick sat down, got a ton of chips, and then immediately asked if we could take a ten-minute break before we got started. I said sure, why not? Then he turned to Molly and asked her if Tobey had left the hotel yet, and Molly assured him he had.

Next thing I know Rick's got a big silver platter from somewhere and has chopped out several massive lines of cocaine on it. And we're not talking sissy little party-girl lines either, these were fat Hollywood rails. Then, with a grin and a wink, he lowered his head and proceeded to snort every fucking one of them by himself.

Rick Salomon didn't fuck around when it came to going off the deep end. The reason he had asked if Tobey had left was that he knew better than to try and pull that shit in front of Spider-Man. Rick was supposed to be sober—Tobey kicked him out of his house once just for walking in with a damn beer. Molly was similar: even though she wouldn't do blow in front of me or Tobey, everybody knew she was matching Rick line for line from the bathroom. The game had just gotten seriously dark.

I declined the offer to join them, splashed some water on my face, stared at my reflection in the mirror, and resolved to play the best damn poker of my life. I was tired as hell, but I was determined to bust Rick for everything he had.

Rick and I had known each other for a while at this point and had played a lot of big posts together. I had even done some business with him—nothing involving naked hotel heiresses unfortunately; instead, I went in with him on a project to send a crew to Thailand to shoot extreme Thai prison fights. Typically, of course, when I got the footage back it was 300 hours of complete vacation footage including Rick partying with Thai girls, watching them drink wine and eat bugs. Whatever else he may have been, Rick knew how to enjoy himself, that's for sure.

How hard could Rick Salomon party? Try this. One night I got a random text from him telling me he was having a "going away" party and that I should come over right away.

I got there and walked into the shadiest Hollywood scene I'd ever encountered. The place was crammed with all kinds of party girls and trust-fund kids doing drugs and having sex all over Rick's house. As I made my way upstairs to find him, I even ran into a bunch of people who worked for me on a TV series I was producing at the time. This girl who was one of my employees was snorting blow off of some dude's abs who had his shirt up and a bunch of baby oil all over his body. It was weird as hell. When she saw me she froze for a minute and then started laughing and pointing at me, saying, "Holy fuck, that's my boss!" I just walked on by and then had someone fire her the next day.

When I got upstairs Rick was sitting on a couch at the top of his balcony wearing this shiny boxer's robe and not much else. Sitting next to him were two beautiful classy-looking women. I say "classy"—but as I got closer I saw one of them was holding a crack pipe up to Rick's lips while the other was lighting it for him. What the fuck?

Even for Salomon this was something else. I said to him, "Bro, why in the fuck are you smoking crack?" and he just laughed (his laugh always sounded like a little kid who had just stolen something and gotten away with it).

"I'm smokin' a bunch of crack tonight," he giggled, "cos I'm going into fuckin' rehab tomorrow in Malibu!"

I asked the girls to leave us alone for a minute and sat next to him with the half-assed idea of talking him out of developing a crack habit, on top of everything else. We were interrupted by the most stunning brunette I had ever seen: she walked up to him and said: "Hey Rick, I'm Joy. We don't know each other but I just wanted to say . . . nice cock!"

On that note I had lost Rick's attention, if I ever had it in the first place. I got out of there . . . and until this night, thought nothing the dude could do would ever surprise me again. I was wrong.

Rick was clearly back on the blow big time again, but this time he had a shitload of money sitting in front of him and I was in desperate need of a huge score to get back to even for the night. This was my chance. I wanted to bust Salomon so bad he would have to add Gambler's Anonymous to his rehab speed-dial list.

We started playing and it seemed my luck was still fucked. Rick was catching cards left and right. It was sick. The only good thing was that he was so out of his mind he was completely incapable of sustaining a bluff and his tells were telegraphed: as well as all the cocaine, throughout the night I watched him pop an entire bottle of powerful yellow Norco pain pills, crunching them like they were M&Ms. I mean . . . this would be enough drugs to kill a mere mortal! But not Rick Salomon!

Silver linings: he may have been riding the cards, but at least his being so fucked up meant I was losing the absolute minimum every time he had a good hand. I knew it was just a matter of time. If I waited him out, he would eventually bluff into the wrong hand and I'd bust him wide open. Rick's a dangerous player, but nobody can get this fucked up and expect to come out on top.

Hours went by, and the sun was up. By then the massage girls had gone home, and Molly had changed out of her skimpy hostess outfit to her usual after-hours sweats and a tank top with no bra and was crashed out on the couch. Manny could barely keep his eyes open to deal, and I was about as tired as I've ever been in my life. Rick, of course, was wide awake and loving life. I held on, kept playing, kept praying.

Finally I picked up the best hand I'd seen in hours. Ace, queen suited. We had hiked the blinds up to $1,000/$2,000 at this point, so the game had the potential to play huge on any given hand. I popped it to forty grand preflop. Rick looked at his hand. Based on how he had been reacting to his cards all night, I could tell he had absolutely nothing. But he smiled, cackled, and called anyway to see a flop.

The flop came queen, seven, deuce—rainbow, meaning three different suits. I knew top pair had him absolutely crushed, so I checked to see if he would bluff at it. Sure enough, he bet $50k and I raised it to $100k figuring that would be the end of it. Rick looked at his cards and tossed his chips into the pot. One of his $25k chips went flying across the table and hit Molly in the face. I had him on squadoosh!

Now wide awake, Molly had left the sofa and was watching the hand go down. This could be my moment! The turn came and it was another rag! A four of clubs. There wasn't even a backdoor flush draw out there. Sure, I would rather have a set, but a winner is a winner and in that sense, this hand was what I'd been waiting all goddamn night for. I breathed deep and bet out $120k. Rick took the bait, raised all-in for the rest of his chips, and I snap called him.

"You got me," he said. Manny dealt a pointless five on the river, and I started to scoop the pot. And that's when Rick turned over his cards and started laughing.

Time stopped. I stared at the board for what seemed like forever. The maniac had called preflop with absolutely nothing—a three and six, off suit. On the flop he found a two and on the turn he picked up a four, somehow setting him up for a miraculous fucking gut shot straight draw . . . and then the lucky bastard hit it on the river. I wanted to fucking kill him.

Finally I stammered, "Rick . . . what were you thinking?" and with that famous Rick Salomon laugh he said, "I was gonna bluff you on the turn, but then I picked up a gut shot and decided I wanted to see the river, so I shoved to give myself some equity if you called me!"

I was shell-shocked. I had just made one of the best reads of my life to have it all blow up in my face. I looked down at my phone and saw a whole series of texts from Bonnie asking me when I would be home. By this time she was already at the Polo Lounge with Tobey's wife, Jen, and was looking forward to whatever plans I had made for that evening. Blood started rushing to my head.

I had just lost a million dollars.

I walked out of the Four Seasons in a daze, somehow made it into my car, and drove home on autopilot. I was so disoriented, so numbed, that it's a wonder I ever made it back at all.

On the drive home Tobey called me and said, "I heard what happened and I just wanted to make sure you haven't driven off a cliff!" I knew in some small way he shared my pain.

Just a few minutes after I got home, Bonnie arrived with the girls. Callie was asleep, but Chloe came running into my arms, screaming, "Daddy, Daddy!" I held her tight and finally, uncontrollably, broke down in tears.

I didn't know what I was going to do. I had been reinvesting most of my money into my business, with the rest barely covering the mortgage on my three-million-dollar house that was now worth only a million due to the market crash, the car payments, and paying off about fifty grand a month on my wife's credit card bill. My business was fucked, Las Vegas hadn't been kind to me, even the neighbors' damn tree was against me . . . and now this. A million bucks in a single night. My entire liquid bankroll wiped out, just like that. I was completely fucked, and there was only one person on Earth who I could turn to that would understand what had just happened to me.

I needed Spider-Man!

Needless to say, I never made it to dinner for my wife's birthday that night. Fortunately for me, Bonnie had a deeper understanding about the world of gambling than most girls who grew up in Beverly Hills—given the fact that she was the daughter of one of the greatest football handicappers in the world.

So instead of celebrating with the love of my life like I should have been doing, I dried my eyes, steadied my breathing, put on my most positive voice, and called Tobey. He told me to head on over and we could discuss the mess I was in.

Tobey and I had started this whole thing, he knew how much money I had made in the game, and with all we'd been through and the history we had playing side by side, I was praying that he would at least hear me out.

I made him a great offer. If he loaned me the million to pay off the debt, I would pay him back with 50 percent of my wins until the debt was clean, and then free roll him on 10 percent of my wins for another year with no exposure on my losses.

If Tobey was anything, he was a negotiator. And big numbers didn't scare him: word was that between *Spider-Man* and *Spider-Man 3* he'd talked the studios up from a straight four million for the first movie to $15 million plus 7.5 percent of the backend for the third film in the franchise. And he wasn't about to fuck around with me: he heard me out and then came straight to his bottom line. He told me he would give me $600k and I would pay him back 50 percent of my wins until that was paid off, then he wanted 50 percent of my wins for another year with no exposure on my losses.

I said "Bro . . . do you know how insane that is?"

Tobey just smiled. "Yep," he said. "And I'm sure you can get better terms from your boys in Vegas, but I will cut you a check right now."

What could I do? He had me over a barrel. Despite the fact that he was gouging me on the deal, there was no way I was turning to Vegas and borrowing mobbed-up money to pay this off. After all, I didn't want to be owing a fucking gangster and I certainly didn't want it getting out that I was hurting. And at least with Tobey giving me the loan, I knew he would be incentivized to keep me in the game.

We scratched out the terms on a napkin with a sharpie and both signed it. Then Tobey reached into his pocket and handed me a check for $600k, easy as that. The sly bastard was so sure I'd take his deal he had written the check before I even got there. Then we shook hands and he joyfully shouted, "I own you now! And I'm gonna make soooo much fucking money this year at poker!"

I've thought about that little outburst a lot since. You could say it was another example of Tobey's dark side, that same narcissism and need for control that had him insist Molly bark like a seal for tips . . . and perhaps it was. But then, honestly, how many people do you know who would write you a six hundred-thousand-dollar check on the spot using a napkin as the contract? Regardless of the terms, he was a stand-up guy for that at least—and that loan truly meant a lot to me.

It was a Saturday and I wanted to get the check deposited immediately, so I shot out of Tobey's place like a rocket and made my way to City National Bank before it closed. Every time I walked into that place, the girls behind the counter would always smile and start whispering to one another. I'd like to think it was over my rugged good looks, but the truth is, they all wondered who the fuck I was. I mean, these girls had seen six-figure checks of mine written from Tobey, Ben Affleck, Jeffrey Katzenberg, Gabe Kaplan, movie directors Todd Phillips and Steve Brill, James Woods, Hank Azaria, rapper Nelly . . . the list was a mile long—not to mention close to a million in checks from Brad Ruderman alone! But today was the day that one of the girls broke down and finally asked me what I did for a living.

I immediately replied with my standard answer: "I'm a producer." But then as I was walking out, for some reason I turned back around and said, "I also play a little poker."

When I got home I called Molly and got a list of who I owed money to from the previous game. By the length of the list you could really tell that I threw the fucking party that night. I sucked it up and used Tobey's 600 and another $400k of my own money to finally pay off what, to that point at least, was the worst night of my life.

If I had been feeling pressure before, now the heat was on more than ever. I woke up thinking about the game, went to the office thinking about the game, and even dreamed about cards and bad beats every time I went to sleep like some twisted recurring nightmare from hell.

Despite all that, for the next three weeks I played the best poker of my life. Every decision was made with pinpoint accuracy. Every call, every bluff, every laydown was dead on. I was on fire. I went into each game knowing that I simply couldn't afford to lose and then somehow turned that fear into faith. Faith in myself and in my decisions at the table. By my third week since the million-dollar loss, a flat-out miracle had happened.

I won enough to pay Tobey back in full! I stared my million-dollar loss in the face and made it my bitch! It was an incredible feeling. For a split second, I felt like I was back and that nothing could stop me! But then I came back to reality when I started thinking about the deal I had made with Tobey.

After getting Tobey paid back, I had to contend with the terms of the deal. For example, if I won a hundred grand, I'd keep $50k and the other $50k would go to Tobey . . . then let's say I win another hundred grand the week after that, same again: fifty each to me and Tobey. So far so good, right? But let's assume the following week I lose a hundred grand. Tobey has no exposure— he's still up $100,000 . . . whereas I, on the other hand, have just lost all of my profit for the last three weeks.

Tobey's generosity had saved my ass for a little while, but the ongoing terms of our deal was crippling me. And if that weren't enough for me to worry about, he was finally ready to fire Molly Bloom once and for all and set up our game at an entirely new location . . . and for God only knows what amount.

It's funny. You lose a million dollars in a single night of poker and you think that's about as bad as things can get. And then you find you're about to be proved wholly, catastrophically, wrong.

CHAPTER 11

THIS IS THE WAY THE WORLD ENDS

At this point I shouldn't have kept playing. I should have immediately bowed out for a year until my deal was up with Tobey. But
if I did that, I knew I would never play in the game again . . . so I
sucked it up, planned for the worst, and hoped for the best. The
one thing I could count on with Molly was the fact that she did
work her ass off to make sure the pond was stocked with fish
every week and that they were always good for their debt.

But all of that was about to change forever . . . And it all began
with a New York hedge fund millionaire who knew just enough
about poker to be dangerous.

One night not long after settling my debt to Tobey, he and I
arrived as usual to find "Hedge Fund" Cliff from New York had
shown up and was eager to play. Cliff was loaded and could be a
maniac with the cards, so we knew the night could get interesting.

And so it did. Within about an hour he and Dave Garden got
into a $750,000 pot where Cliff went runner runner for a miracle
full house with ace king after Dave had flopped a boat with pocket
queens. To this day it was one of the sickest hands I've ever seen.
For those of you who are scratching your heads right now, the
board was queen, 7, 7. Dave was holding pocket queens. A Full
house! And Cliff was holding ace, king . . . not even a pair! Cliff
bluffs all of his money off to Dave, who of course calls. Now, to

hit one ace on the turn was one thing, but to hit two aces in a row . . . well, the odds were in the thousands. To make matters worse, this was the game where Dave had promised to tip twenty grand to the dealer if he won a pot over $300k and five grand to the girl who was massaging his feet. That's right . . . these guys were playing for millions of dollars while getting a foot massage!

Cliff had maniacked his way into an absolute miracle. If this hand ever made it to TV, it would be one of the all-time worst beats in the history of televised poker. Did that mean Cliff walked away an even richer man? No! Later that night Bobby Safi made a hero call against him to bust him in a pot that was over $800k. Cliff just laughed like it was no big deal.

So far, so fun. But it was at the end of the night as we were all chatting that Tobey dropped the bomb. "You know what, Cliff," he said, "you should hire Molly to run your game in New York."

And just like that it was over. The beautiful little hustle Spider-Man and I cooked up in his kitchen to hustle LA's idle rich and the Hollywood elite might have grown into a vicious beast I could barely control . . . but up till then it had still been our plan, our hustle, our beast. And no matter how betrayed I feel by her now, I must admit, Molly Bloom had played a part of that.

Of course, the way she tells it, Tobey just cut her loose over a phone call rather than actually securing her a job. But the truth is, by recommending her to Cliff like that, he figured he'd come up with the perfect way to both get rid of her and do it in a way that actually helped the girl get on. It's like the corporate office giving you a promotion but making you move to the East Coast to assume your new duties. Everyone wins.

To this day, it makes me queasy thinking about how badly she portrayed us in her book and film. We made her rich!

That was all to come, however. Right then Miss Bloom was no longer my problem. She reluctantly took the gift that Tobey gave her and split for the Big Apple. She was gone, and for all I knew I would never see her again. I now had to deal with the fact that the game was about to change in a big way, and I wasn't sure what my role was going to be from this point forward.

The next day, Tobey and I got together to discuss our next moves. He told me that the following week's game was going to be held at Alec Gores's new megamansion. He was superexcited about it because Alec was a big fish and could afford to lose millions to us without it affecting him whatsoever—the way Tobey saw it, having a whale like that hosting the whole operation only meant better fishing for him.

I wasn't so sure. While I agreed with Tobey on many levels, I always had a slightly different opinion about Alec. There are players who will never go broke and never get any better, like Hedge Fund Cliff . . . but then there are the kind of players who look at the game as an investment. When you start up a business you can't always expect to be profitable out of the gate. Sometimes you have to invest a lot of dough before the company begins to make a bit back in return.

Well, Alec Gores owned 90 companies at the time . . . and from what I heard, he made a fortune on every damn one of them. And with Alec planning to now hold our weekly game in his 50,000-square-foot Beverly Park megamansion, I couldn't help but wonder what his long-term play was. Until now, Alec had been a huge loser at poker, but he was the biggest winner out of all of us in terms of business . . . and if anyone understood the phrase "speculate to accumulate," it was him.

The first night at Alec's mansion was unreal. If I thought we'd been living the high life before then, his place made the other game venues look like skid row. I picked up Tobey and we made our way up to Beverly Park, an elite gated community full of ridiculous wealth. Alec's newly built home there was literally like a castle. The main house was over 40,000 square feet, and there was a 10,000-square-foot guesthouse on the property occupied by one of Alec's children.

As we made our way into the giant dome-shaped foyer, we were greeted by a butler who escorted us to the wing of the house that held the billiard room, the movie theater, the three-story, 2,600-bottle wine cellar . . . and, of course, the custom-built poker room. We were also told that dinner would be catered by Mistral, one of Mr. Gores's favorite restaurants.

That first night Alec was the perfect host. The setup felt like our normal weekly game except we'd upgraded from luxury hotel to billionaire's palace. At dinnertime we went upstairs to his gourmet kitchen and dining area to find that our meals were not only catered by Mistral, but that the restaurant's owner, Henry, was there to personally set up the table. Alec then pointed out that this kitchen was for his "personal use" when he wanted to make his own sandwich or grab a drink from the fridge. Otherwise he had a full-time chef and waiting staff who worked primarily in the other kitchen, which was built like that of a large five-star restaurant and could serve hundreds of people a day if need be.

Jeez: how the other half live, right? In famous LA fashion, we all just shrugged and gave polite compliments as if this level of wealth and opulence were normal.

There are two other things I will never forget about that night. One was the fact that baseball superstar A-Rod was there but only wanted to watch. Apparently he had got interested in poker, but had never played, so Alec invited him to see what the game was like. It was pretty bizarre seeing this huge star idolized by millions watching with wide eyes like an awestruck schoolboy at all of the money flying around the room.

The other thing was distinctly more ominous. When Manny went on a break, Alec had another dealer there as well, and on her very first hand something strangely familiar seemed to be afoot. Remember my story about the cooler and the stacked hand I dubbed the Saint Valentine's Day Massacre? Well . . . it sure seemed like a similar situation, only this time, I wasn't the one behind the scenes.

I was in late position and looked down at pocket jacks. But by the time the betting had got 'round to me, the pot had been raised, reraised, and had two callers. There had to be close to $500k in the middle, and given the financial situation I was in and the deal I'd struck with Tobey I couldn't imagine my pocket jacks were worth the risk, so I mucked them.

Not everybody was so cautious, however. Kevin Washington called behind me, Alec went all-in, I think Tobey mucked, but everyone else at the table called until it got around to Kevin again. He looked at his hand and said, "Fuck it . . . I'm all-in, too!"

When the cards got turned over I couldn't believe my eyes. Alec turned over his hand first to show pocket aces, then came pocket 10s, pocket queens, and pocket kings! Unbelievable. And perhaps the least surprising thing about it was the fact that maniac Kevin had called with a king and a six of spades.

No sets hit the board, but by some kind of miracle K-Wash (as we called him) managed to river a spade flush to take the entire pot. And I think that might have been the only thing that kept me from overthinking the weirdness of the hand too much. Kevin obviously wasn't supposed to call, and Alec would have won in a historical way with at least a Quadruple Duke, as we like to say in the card hustling business.

I should have stood up and walked then. I mean, what kind of game deals 10 10, JJ, KK, QQ, and AA? If I saw that in a movie I would laugh it off as impossible; if I was told about it by another card player I'd mark him down as drunk, or a bullshitter, or both. Hell, I wasn't even that aggressive the time I rung in a cooler to bust the Armenians in Glendale!

Even if a cold deck had been slipped into the game that was prestacked, I never would have arranged it to be consecutive pair over pair. Maybe that was the wild genius of it—it was so blatant a hustle it could only have been a genuinely freak occurrence: I guess that's why everyone shrugged it off and carried on.

I won a couple hundred grand that night—though of course it was really only a net win of a single hundred because I owed Tobey 50 percent. But he had a great night as well and on the way home told me to hold onto it for my bankroll and that we would just keep track of my wins from here on out. He had already been paid back the $600k loan he gave me . . . so everything from this point on was gravy for him. We'd put his percentage on a tab and both agreed I could pay him down the road after I had booked a few million in wins. Once again, Maguire had shown me how much of a stand-up guy he really was: sure, he got the best of it on our financial deal . . . but he wasn't being a vulture about it. He wanted to see me do well and rebuild my bankroll back to what it had gotten up to by the end of 2007.

Alec's house became our new spot, and soon it was as if Molly Bloom had never even existed. The first three weeks I played there, I averaged a $200,000-dollar-per-night win. In less than a month I already had over $300k on Tobey's tab, and I'd all but put the freak hand of that first night behind me.

I shouldn't have. Alec the business shark was still speculating to accumulate. And he was about to show his teeth. The power dynamic had shifted, and our hustle was about to enter its endgame.

When we showed up the fourth week, there was no sign of Manny. Instead, Alec had replaced him completely with his own dealers, one of whom was the girl who had dealt that crazy hand on the first night. Another looked like a Maxim model (hell, I think she *was* a Maxim model), but she obviously knew her way around the poker room. I had never seen her before at any other games and was curious how Alec found her. But the biggest surprise of all was the fact that Alec had invited cash poker pros Kenny Tran and David Peat—a.k.a. "Viffer," as he is known in the poker world.

I looked at Tobey expecting him to be just as suspicious as I was about this, but he seemed to be all smiles. I think Spidey was looking for more of a challenge to his game at this point and welcomed the competition. Why not? He could afford to.

I, on the other hand, had absolutely no desire to get mixed up in pots with either of these guys. Viffer was known to go off the rails now and again, but he was a dangerous opponent . . . and Kenny Tran? Kenny has been making a living playing poker against pros at the Commerce for over half his life. He's a monster player, and in my opinion, neither of them had any business being in a soft game like this. Apart from anything else, this was my cherry patch! This was the game Tobey and I had built from the ground up, hustle after hustle. At least, it was supposed to be. Now I wasn't so sure.

That night, nothing too out of the ordinary seemed to happen. Kenny played supertight, and Viffer played superloose and aggressive, but I avoided getting mixed up in pots with him and instead let him go after guys like Bob Safi. He also put Tobey to the test on a pretty big bluff, but Tobey called him for a six-figure pot. Aside from that, at the end of the night, both Viffer and Tran had lost money to our host. Alec was up about $300k and felt on top of the world.

What in hell was going on? Tobey may have been content, but my spider senses were tingling. How could two high-stakes cash pros dump to Alec like this? They were either playing out of their comfort zone, which was unlikely, or else they were working the long game and wanting Alec to think he could bust them every week so they would get invited back. But maybe there was also a third option.

I pondered for two days straight before it finally it hit me. Alec had to be staking these guys! Gores was treating the game just like he does his leveraged buyouts. He comes in, he takes over, and then he makes a profit. How could we have been so blind to this?

It made perfect sense. Alec had Viffer, Tran, or perhaps both of them playing for him. That would explain them dumping to him the first night but also giving Alec a good excuse to invite them both back in case anyone else objected. And what could we say? Alec not only won money off these guys; the whole game was now centered around his hospitality . . . I couldn't just step up and demand they be uninvited.

Looking back, my intuition about Alec Gores was right from the very beginning. I never thought of him as a long-term sucker, and he was proving me right. I believe he had both of these guys staked for a big percentage and planned on winning back every dollar he had ever lost playing poker with us. Technically, a little collusion on this level isn't necessarily considered "cheating," but it's certainly what I would call "gaining the advantage."

And let's face it, when it came to making money, Alec had been playing the angles in order to gain the advantage his whole god-damn life. Why would he stop with poker?

What could I do? The truth was—nothing, nada, zilch. Molly may have had her faults and God knows I'm no fan of hers these days, but the truth is after she had gone and Alec started hosting, Tobey and I lost control of the very game we started. If I wanted to even stay a part of it, then all I could do was play along and sweat out each game like some kind of Hollywood Park grinder.

Despite it all, I figured there were still other fish to be had. Brad Ruderman was still in the game, and he was always good for a six-figure loss. All I had to do was avoid Kenny and Viffer and I should be all right. And that's the attitude I had when I arrived at the game the next week.

Things started well. I was happy to see Manny back in the dealer's chair at the beginning of the night. With Ruderman in the game and a dealer I trusted, I expected to have a solid night as usual.

We were a couple hours in when Alec said something that was to change my life forever—and finally kill Hollywood's greatest hustle stone dead. Not that anyone realized at the time: he just mentioned to Brad Ruderman that his financial team was liqui-dating some of his hedge fund investments and that he would need to get the $10 million (plus profit) back from Brad that he had invested with him. Brad assured him it would be no big deal and that he would have it to him by the end of the week.

And that, boys and girls, is the way the world ends. Not with a bang . . . but a conversation.

But I didn't realize it at the time—I was more worried about the fact that I couldn't catch a hand to save my life, despite how bad my good pal Bobby Safi tried to give me money. In one hand I got him to invest $60k preflop when I had pocket aces. Then, just to avoid a bad beat and take the money after the flop came 9, 5, deuce, I turned the aces face up, moved all-in, and told Bobby to throw his hand in the muck. Instead, Bobby basically gave me the finger and snap called my all-in with fucking 9,10 off suit. And of course he hit a miracle 9 on the turn to once again pour scorn on the odds and crack my aces wide open. It was moments like this that made me wish I was dealing the cards and controlling the outcome like I had spent so many thousands of hours learning how to do throughout my life.

I was so heated I literally had to go outside and cool off for 10 minutes. When I came back, I immediately lost another pot to Rick Salomon flush over flush.

Was history about to repeat itself? Not this time. I did the smart thing, called it a night, and decided to leave before I got myself on tilt. Whoever was owed money when the game was over would call me and I would meet up with them the next day. I walked away that night $300k down: the exact amount that Tobey was owed off of my wins for the past few weeks.

The next day, I got a call from Kenny Tran. He told me that Rick Salomon owed him a hundred grand from the game, but he would rather collect from me because he had some reason to believe Rick was gonna slow pay him. Truth is, I imagine he owed Rick money from a sports bet and was trying to get to me before anyone else did so he wouldn't have to deal with Rick.

I met up with Kenny at the Beverly Hills Hotel and gave him a check for the hundred. That's when he told me he had worked it out so that the entire $300k loss of mine needed to go to him. I told him I would call him in a day or so.

The next day, Manny the dealer came to see me. He told me something that sent chills down my spine. One of the pros Alec had invited into the game (and I won't say which one) had approached him with new decks of cards they wanted him to use. That's when I knew that the fix was in. The fuckers weren't even trying to be subtle about it. I've been around the block enough to know that when a player tries to insert new decks into a game, it's never a good sign. Personally, I believe he was trying to slip in a juice deck that was loaded with an infrared marking system on the back of every card—invisible except to infrared contact lenses or glasses.

Shit was heading way out on a limb, and sadly, I found myself on the wrong side of the hustle. The game Tobey and I had begun five or so years ago may have been pitched to take millions off Hollywood's rich and careless from the start . . . and sure, I may have run the occasional unbeatable prop bet or stacked a showdown here and there . . . but for the most part, we always beat the game straight up. There was a kind of camaraderie about it, a bond we shared, an adventure we were all on together. And we never, ever, cheated.

I knew where the game was heading. It was becoming a gigantic version of the games I hustled when I was younger and completely fearless. This is when things have the potential to get ugly in more ways than one.

I stopped playing and instead spent a few weeks sampling smaller, less respectable games. Hell, at one point I even took a job for a flat fee win or lose. This guy paid me a few grand to play as a shill in his game: I won $30k for him that night but only went home with $3,000 for myself.

Despite it all, a part of me still hoped things weren't as irretrievably fucked as they seemed. Perhaps Alec's game would straighten itself out and I would eventually make my way back to it without having to rat anyone out for what I suspected to be a pretty big scam going on.

After all, I may be many things, but I've never been a rat. And while I really wanted to go to Tobey and tell him what I had learned, I chose to just keep my mouth shut. As for Manny . . . he refused to ring in the cooler and eventually lost his job for Alec completely.

Did Gores know what was going on? I'm pretty sure not. He saw the guys he was inviting as professionals, and if he did have a financial arrangement with them, he would just assume he was making his money through them honestly. There's just no need for a guy like Alec to knowingly get involved with marked cards.

I never did play in the big game again. I decided to kind of check out from poker for a while and take a long hard look at my life. Then one morning I got a call from Dave Garden telling me that Brad Ruderman had been arrested.

Alec had given Ruderman a week to get his $10 million, and when no money showed up, and Brad wasn't at the next game, he got suspicious. The week after that, the Feds raided Ruderman's office to find that the fucker had been turning dollars into dimes for over a year and that his $50 million hedge fund had about $500k left in it. That half-mill, a couple of Porsches, and his place in Malibu were immediately confiscated, and Brad was hauled off to prison.

If it was a shocker, at first I thought to myself: damn . . . at least I dodged that bullet. The value of my house had tanked, my business was in turmoil, and my poker career had suddenly come to a halt, but at least Brad's bullshit didn't touch me directly.

That's when I received notice that a $750,000 lien had been put on my house over the Ruderman scandal. For those lucky enough never to have come across the word, a lien is a legal term denoting the right given to another to secure a debt.

The Feds were coming for everyone in the game who had ever received a check from Bad Brad. It was a long list that included Tobey, Nick Cassavetes, Ben Affleck, Rick Salomon, Dave Garden, Bob Safi, Mike Baxter, Bosko, Alec Gores, and a slew of others. Sadly, I was at the top of that list, as I had taken more checks from Ruderman than almost anyone else in the game aside from maybe Bob Safi. But how in the hell would the Feds even know that all of that money Brad lost went to settle his poker debts? Molly Bloom, that's how! The Feds had applied just the tiniest bit of pressure to Molly, and she rolled over like a puppy and gave us all up. My attorney got hold of her deposition, which gave every detail of our poker game dating all the way back to The Viper Room. The first name mentioned in the depo? Houston Curtis.

Thanks to Molly's cooperation with the Feds, they came after me for around $750k. Dave Garden had a high number too, Tobey had received about $300k . . . hell, we had all taken our piece of flesh, and now, in a bizarre twist, the bankruptcy courts had exploited a loophole that allowed them to come after every dollar Ruderman had paid to us based on the fact that he had been stealing the money from his hedge fund to pay us what he'd lost at the game.

In other words, legally speaking, the money was never his in the first place—and therefore they could take it back off us. To make it even more rock solid for them, Molly handed over all of her fucking spreadsheets detailing every single transaction.

Talk about a bad beat! Of course everyone lawyered up and was starting to settle. I got a call from Alec "The Billionaire"'s office asking me if I wanted to join Alec and a bunch of the other guys in a joint defense. Alec agreed to pay the first $70k in legal bills and after that, it would have to be split amongst us.

I figured I didn't have anything to lose, so I agreed: in fact, given the financial straits I was in, plus the $750k I supposedly now had to find to pay back money I had legitimately won at the time, I didn't exactly have much choice.

Guess what. They must have been some pretty damn high-priced attorneys because after two conference calls the $70k retainer was spent! And that's when I noticed the fine print of our agreement. Apparently Alec's attorneys had structured it in a way where whoever took the most money off of Brad would have to bear the most amount of financial responsibility to the attorneys to negotiate a settlement. Me, in other words.

Fuck that! I wasn't about to settle, let alone pay the lion's share of attorneys' fees just to help out a bunch of multimillionaires for whom a couple hundred grand amounted to little more than chump change.

I dropped out and let the bastards come after me. What the hell, my house was eventually gonna go into foreclosure seeing as how the value had dropped from three million to one million . . . and now with another $750,000 lien on top of that, I was totally screwed every which way. Not to mention, Alec was on both sides of this thing. Sure, he received a few bucks from Ruderman in the game . . . but Alec was also one of the investors the bankruptcy court was trying to collect the money for. Talk about a conflict of interest. The entire situation smelled like a Montana Shoeshine.

Sadly, it had come to the point where I needed to call in my insurance policy. My father-in-law, my mentor, Mr. B. He was my nuclear option, but, finally, I had no choice. With a heavy heart I sat down with him and explained my situation. He was a total badass who had beaten the system his whole life and now he was gonna save his son-in-law's ass, right?

At first he told me not to worry. Then when I brought it up to him again, he didn't remember us even talking about it the first time. Within a few months we realized that my father-in-law had full-blown Alzheimer's and it was getting worse by the week. It was truly heartbreaking seeing someone who had been such a mentor deteriorating in front of my eyes. I'll never forget talking to him and seeing his eyes water. This was a tough-as-nails guy who had depended on his wits his entire life. And I could tell that he would never be the same.

And just like that I had nobody to save me. This is the way the world ends: not with a bang but a conversation.

My first thought was not for myself, but for my poor wife, Bonnie. She had grown up a child of privilege, never having to want for anything. Then she married a man much like her father who made sure she still never had to want for anything. And now she was about to find out not only that her husband was broke, but that her father was also in dire straits. She didn't deserve this.

CHAPTER 12

DEUS EX MACHINA, MOTHERFUCKER

The game was dead. The perfect little hustle Tobey and I had cooked up in his kitchen, grown in The Viper Room, and seen blossom so beautifully in the most luxurious hotels in Los Angeles had fallen apart, wracked and ruined by a grim trinity of greed, bad luck, and its own success. After so painstakingly putting together the ultimate "gentlemen's game," it only took one snake, Ruderman, and one scorned woman, Molly Bloom, to bring it all to a screeching halt. Now Molly was long gone, Bad Brad was behind bars, and the world's greatest poker game would never be the same again.

But it wasn't over. For some of us at least, there was further to fall. And I was about to fall deeper and harder than anyone.

Do you remember the term *deus ex machina*? The Latin phrase describes an ancient trick used in classical theater to resolve complicated or seemingly hopeless situations in the plots of their plays. Often the plot devices used would seem extraordinary, outlandish, desperately unlikely. The phrase is loosely translated as "God from the machine."

Well I don't want to overstate the case, but what happened to me next is pure deus ex machina. And my life was to end up like the bad ending of a Greek tragedy.

The poker game I had begun, and that had been supporting my failing business for the past six months, was over. I had made and lost a fortune. My house was worth two million less than when I bought it, and now, thanks to Bad Brad, I had an additional $750k lien to find. I had a feature film I was producing that caused me to borrow money from family and friends in order to finish, and all of the companies who owed me millions of dollars in royalties and distribution fees were going belly-up faster than a rat in a cathouse due to the financial collapse of 2008.

This is about the time my mother would say: "At least you've got your health." Well, guess what.

Greek tragedies don't just end with the demise of the leading man—more often than not a whole host of others wind up in the shit, too.

My father-in-law's aggressive form of Alzheimer's disease was only getting worse. I wanted to go to his two oldest sons, Fred and Andy, and clue them in on what was happening with their father, but Bonnie's dad was too proud and had strongly forbidden me or Bonnie from sharing any of his problems with his other children.

It hurt, but I had to respect the guy. Then, out of nowhere, Bonnie's mother was diagnosed with a rare lung disease and she flew back to Boston, along with Bonnie, my daughters, and Mr. B, where she was admitted to Salem Hospital.

I was left in LA trying to hold it altogether and at the same time looking to sell a show or make a deal fast in order to stay afloat.

My agents had set up multiple pitches for a slew of reality shows I was developing, and a lot of those pitches took place on the East Coast. At this point, I couldn't even afford a plane ticket, so I had to borrow money just to attend the meetings. First I went to New York and then on to Washington, DC, where I was going to meet with Discovery Channel and a few of their subsidiary cable partners.

The night before my meeting with Discovery, I woke up gasping for air. I was sweating through the bedsheets, my heart flailing, my breath coming in tiny raggedy bursts, as if I were trying to breathe through a straw. At first I thought it was an anxiety attack . . . except it happened all night long.

But what could I do? I was broke, here in DC on borrowed money, and if I didn't close a deal, things were only going to get worse. I didn't have time for this shit. I had to keep going.

I managed to make it through the night, and the next day I walked the two blocks to the Discovery Channel building. By the time I got there, I felt like I was going to die. I could hardly breathe, my whole body burned, it was all I could do to keep from hyperventilating. Somehow I made it through the pitches and promised myself I would see a doctor as soon as I was back in LA.

I got home very late. Bonnie and the girls were in Boston, so the house was very quiet. I went to turn the lights on and . . . nothing. The power had been shut off. The hot water was turned off, as well. Seems I owed about $17,000 on water and power bills, and they had simply shut everything off while I was away. Foreclosure notices and past-due bills were piling up in the mailbox. I don't think I had even opened a bill in years. I usually paid someone to do that for me.

The next day I called my buddy Jerome Seven, who's like an old-school MacGyver kind of dude, and within minutes he had the power back on and the water heater, as well. We shared a laugh at that—we'd struck one small blow back against the Universe.

The Universe had other ideas. That evening I once again woke up gasping for air. I ended up passing out on the floor in my bedroom and came to an hour later, shaking and scared shitless.

When I woke up, I also noticed that my legs, ankles, and feet had swollen up to at least three times their normal size. I called a close family friend, Jason Gordon Thomas, whose family started the St. Jude's Children's Hospital, and he came over right away to take me to the ER.

As soon as the nurses saw how swollen my feet were, they got me on a gurney and wheeled me into the Emergency Room. The next few hours were spent running all kinds of tests without ever determining just what was wrong with me. During all this they noticed two spots on my chest that they thought could be cancerous, so while I was there they wanted to do a biopsy just to be safe.

Just before going in for surgery, they ran one more test to see if they could determine the cause of my symptoms. They put a bunch of jelly on my chest above my heart and started pressing down on it using the same kind of device they used on my wife to check on her when she was pregnant.

I saw the nurse trying to hold back a huge gasp as she looked at the results. I asked her what the problem was, and she ran out of the room, returning with one of the lead heart surgeons at Cedars-Sinai Hospital. The doctor told me that my heart was very enlarged and my heartbeat had become irregular, to say the least. Given this new information, I assumed they would skip the biopsy, but a half hour later I was being wheeled into the OR. My close friends Mike Nichols, Sam Korkis, and Dave Weidenhoffer had shown up and promised to stick around till the whole thing was done with.

The anesthesiologists asked me to sign a form, and before I knew it I was falling into a deep sleep.

It seemed like I had been out for a long time when all of a sudden the sound in the room hit me as if someone had just turned on a loud stereo. It was pitch-dark and I couldn't open my eyes, but I could hear Van Halen playing and above the music there were what I assumed to be doctors talking about me. Then the voices began to fade slowly into silence again, and the next thing I knew, my eyes were open and I could see people scurrying around the operating room.

The biopsy was supposed to be a simple procedure. An easy in and out.

Apparently not. When I woke I was in a different room altogether. I had a tube stuck down my throat and I was once again gasping for air.

I desperately wanted to tell them to take the tube out of my throat, but my hands were strapped down and I couldn't talk or move. It was like something you would imagine out of a horror movie. Finally, a nurse came over, and after I managed to shake and grunt enough, she gave me a pencil and held a pad of paper by my hand. I scribbled out the words: "Get this fucking tube out of my throat ASAP." That's when she told me that I was in the ICU, and I was lucky to be alive.

Lucky?

If that tube hadn't been jammed down my throat, I would be laughing. Lucky. I'd almost forgotten what it was like to be lucky as I was laying there gasping in one small breath of air about every seven seconds.

An hour later they finally got the tube out of me. The doctor came in and explained that during the biopsy I went into cardiac arrest due to heart failure.

Of course the spot on my chest was completely benign (phew! "Lucky," right?), but now I had much bigger problems. I was diagnosed with cardiomyopathy. Heart disease. Fuck.

I really didn't know what any of it meant at first, but I would later learn that just 25 percent of patients diagnosed with my condition will respond favorably to treatment. Meaning three in four won't. I've played enough poker to know those odds didn't sound good at all.

But all I wanted to do at that moment was get the hell out of there. Mike and Sam had waited it out, and Jason had been checking up on me, as had my old buddy Dave Weidenhoffer, who originally moved to LA with me and our friend Steve when we were eighteen years old.

And then Bonnie showed up at the hospital, straight from the airport. For a guy who considers himself to be pretty tough, this was finally too much. I just broke down in tears. Our entire world was in chaos. Call me a card hustler, a lowbrow reality TV producer, call me whatever else you like, but one thing I have always been is a provider. I always took care of the people closest to me. Right then, looking at my beautiful, heartbroken wife, I realized, for the first time ever, I couldn't take care of anyone, especially not myself.

And, surely, that's the lowest point, right? That's where, with all the shit out in the open and priorities realized and death dodged, things finally settle down and start to straighten themselves out, no matter how hard the process.

Not a bit of it. Deus ex machina, motherfucker.

While I was fighting for my life in the ICU, the power at my house had been shut off yet again. Seems they'd got wise to our MacGyver tricks, and this time they killed it at the street so we couldn't do anything without settling the bill. To make things worse, I was barely out of hospital when Mrs. B took a bad turn and Bonnie was forced once more to fly back to Boston. Within a few days, my mother-in-law had passed away. Sadly, I never had the chance to say good-bye. She was a beautiful woman who, in her day, was a dead ringer for Jackie Kennedy. Why was all of this happening?

I was under so much damn stress my head was about to explode. I was fresh out of intensive care, still broke, had no power, and needed to get to Boston for my mother-in-law's funeral. So I reached out to an old poker buddy of mine called Nicko who made his living in small private cash games as well as grinding it out at the Commerce. Nick told me he would pay the power bill and give me a few grand in cash if I would let him rent the house out to vacationers while I was in Boston. I thankfully agreed, took the cash, and flew to be by Bonnie's side.

After a very painful funeral we decided it would be best for Bonnie to stay in Boston, where she would at least have access to her family home in Marblehead and help take care of her father, whose Alzheimer's was getting worse every day. Also Chloe and Callie could go to school on the North Shore, where the public-school system rivals the $35k a year I was paying in LA for the girls to go to private school with all of the rich Hollywood elites.

Meanwhile, I flew back to California to try once again to pick up the scattered pieces of my life and deal with my heart condition. The doctors had me on six different medications and a very restrictive diet. At first when they told me there was a 25 percent chance the medication could help me; I didn't realize what the 75 percent chance of it not helping would actually mean for me. It was life and death. And I don't think I was really ready to accept that at this point.

All of the people I considered family were now gone . . . as were the Mercedes and the incredible watch collection I had accumulated over the years. Almost everything I owned had been either pawned, repossessed, or stolen. I thought about reaching out to Tobey, and I even picked up the phone to call him a couple times. But every time I started to dial his number, I would hang up before it rang. I was embarrassed and humiliated. We had been on top of the world together, and now I would be little more than a charity case to him and Leo and the entire crowd that I was once a part of.

The truth is, while their wealth and status kept them insulated even from the Ruderman fallout, I was living in a completely different world now. The last thing I ever wanted to deal with when I was on top was a fucking sob story from someone down on their luck looking for a handout or some kind of sympathy. I didn't call Tobey—partly out of pride, partly out of stubbornness . . . and partly out of kindness. I wanted to spare him the embarrassment of having to talk to me.

In desperation for cash, I pawned just about everything I owned of value. The designer kitchen went—from my Viking fridge, dishwashers, and Wolf oven, down to the light fixtures off the walls. I even tried to sell the island in the kitchen to these Armenian guys, but it was too damn big to be taken out.

Remember the definition of deus ex machina? How the plot device that ties it all up can often be outlandish or desperately unlikely? Well try this one on for size. In the end it wasn't the money that sank me, it wasn't the heart attack that ruined me. It was something even worse.

One day a guy who worked for the company who was trying to buy my house from the bank showed up with a sheriff complaining that I didn't have the right to be gutting it, due to the foreclosure. I asked the sheriff if I was under arrest, and he said, "No sir, this is a domestic matter, we're just here because he called us."

Excellent. I immediately told the officer that this guy was trespassing and I wanted him either thrown off my property or arrested. I'll never forget the fact that my dear friend and former protégé Jeff Kelly was there that day. Jeff had worked for me for years as an editor, and I was letting him use the house for a video shoot. Jeff told the guy to take his stupid frosted-tip haircut and leave before we kicked his ass. It was funny at the time, but any laughter during this tumultuous time was short-lived at best.

The very next day, I was standing on my balcony when all of a sudden I heard someone yell: "Mack Curtis! Put your hands in the air!"

My legal name is Mack Houston Curtis, Mack after my father but anytime someone calls me Mack, it takes me a few seconds to respond because I've always gone by Houston. I looked down from my balcony and standing there, right in the exact same spot where that giant tree had come crashing down on my house so many months before, was a guy dressed in plain street clothes, pointing a gun straight at me.

My mind was racing. Who the fuck would want to shoot me? Those Armenians who I hustled a few years back when I needed to make ends meet? The guy from my apartment block decades ago whose pop-up casino I busted? Somebody from the big game who I wronged in some way?

Then I heard it again, this time saying my full name: "Mack Houston Curtis! We have you surrounded! Come down with your hands up!"

I should have been calm and called an attorney, but instead, I went downstairs and opened the door.

The guy was still holding the gun, dressed like a hood rat. "Mr. Curtis, I'm a detective with LAPD," he said. "Will you please step outside?"

For some reason, I was more worried about the neighbors seeing something weird going down, so I told him I would rather talk to him in the house. To which he replied: "If you will invite me in, we can talk inside." What the fuck . . . was this guy a vampire showing up to drain me of my last drop of blood? He might as well have been.

Not calling my attorney immediately was my first mistake. Allowing him to come in my house was my second mistake. As soon as he got in, he asked if I would let his partner in who was around the back, also with gun drawn. And then without any further discussion, he asked me to turn around, put my hands behind my back, and told me that I was a fugitive from justice out of Las Vegas, Nevada, and they had a warrant for my arrest.

Cut to phase three of my Greek tragedy.

This was a warrant out of Las Vegas over a stupid marker dispute that had happened a while back when I was scrambling for cash on the heels of losing everything. I had been slowly trying to pay it back, but apparently the Green Valley Ranch, an off-strip Vegas casino, had decided to turn it over to the DA, who duly issued a warrant. Until recently, the warrant only covered the state of Nevada but had somehow just gone national. So there I was . . . on top of everything else, fucking arrested.

Have you ever watched one of those shows that highlights the most dangerous prisons in the world? Well if you have, then you will know that LA County Jail is right up there with the very worst of them. It's more dangerous than Pelican Bay, California; or Sing Sing, New York. And suddenly that's where I was headed.

After sitting in a holding cell for six hours at the Van Nuys police department, a guard came in and led me off to a big bus full of what looked like killers, rapists, and terrifying-looking gangbangers and chained me to the guy who was sitting in front of me. This dude had a tattoo on the back of his bald head of a Mexican señorita holding a glock in each hand with the words "FUCK LAPD" written from ear to ear. Needless to say, it was a very unpleasant ride.

I was told we were being taken straight to jail, but the bus made several stops along the way to pick up more criminals. It was hours later by the time we got to the LA County jail, and having never been before I didn't understand why a lot of the guys on the bus were getting so excited.

I soon found out it was because once you arrive at LA County, they give you a microwaved burrito as you walk in. And that would be the first and last thing you would ever want to eat in that place.

Once we got inside, they lined us all up and made us strip naked and empty all of our personal belongings on the floor. Then they ordered us to spread our butt cheeks so they could check up our asses for drugs. Once that humiliation was over, our clothes were put in trash bags and we were given the county blues to wear.

Until that point, I was pretty sure that I had already lost everything that ever meant anything to me. My wife and kids were living almost 3,000 miles away on the opposite coast, my mother-in-law was dead, my father-in-law in the throes of Alzheimer's, my father had passed, and my poor little mother back in Illinois didn't need to know how bad it was, otherwise she'd probably be in the hospital herself due to a stroke or some damn thing. My house was in foreclosure, my business was in the toilet, my heart was apparently fucked, and the poker game that once put me on top of the world was nothing more than a distant memory. But it wasn't until I had to spread my ass cheeks in front of the LAPD standing next to a line of gangbangers, drug dealers, rapists, and robbers that I realized that the one thing I had been holding onto after losing everything else had been my self-respect. And now that was gone, too. What the hell else could they take?

CHAPTER 13

UNLUCKY FOR SOME

Now, I've stood next to people I didn't particularly care for a few times in my life. But I had never been in a situation like this. After arriving in LA County Jail, I was shuffled from one holding cell to another for five straight hours before anyone called my name. And even then all that happened was that I was tossed into another line and made to sit straddle-style on a cold metal bench for another hour with guards yelling, "Nuts to butts, you maggots!" as they jammed us in like sardines before sending us for our official sign-in. It was humiliating. All of the cops looked like gang members themselves.

By the time I was in line for a shower and a bed assignment, 18 hours had gone by. My back was killing me, I hadn't taken any of my heart medication, and I was back in another holding cell that was packed so tight you could barely breathe. Eventually I found a roll of toilet paper and put it under my head like a pillow and tried to take a nap on the piss-stained cold cement floor, a foot away from the only toilet in the place.

Just as I was about to doze off, they opened up the gate and moved us again. This time the holding cell was so small no one could even sit down. Guys were banging on the wall and getting into fights. It was like a scene out of a postapocalyptic film where everyone had gone nuts. Was this a typical Friday night in this place?

The guy next to me kept yelling right in my ear: "Jailer . . . Jailer . . . I need some fuckin' toilet paper . . . " But the jailer never came. Finally he ripped off his T-shirt and sat down on the commode, which was even more filthy and disgusting than the one in my previous holding cell had been. Just as he finished wiping with his shirt, a guard showed up with a roll of toilet paper and a riot almost broke out. The guy who had just wiped his ass on his shirt was losing his mind and started spitting toward the front of the holding cell toward the guard. A big wad of phlegm landed on the back of a Chinese guy's head, and suddenly all hell broke loose.

Ten cops came running in ready for war and swinging. We had been packed so tight I could barely breathe, so I tried to make my way past the cops out of the cell, and suddenly I became extremely light-headed. The last thing I remember hearing before my head hit the ground was somebody yelling at the top of his lungs, "Man, fuck this place!" and I was out.

I came to lying in a prison hospital bed with an IV in my arm. Apparently, not having my medicine combined with the enormous amount of sudden stress had shocked my system. Plus, I hadn't had anything to drink in hours, and aside from my very brief attempt at a nap near an open toilet or the hour I sat nuts to butts on the cold metal rail, I had been on my feet all day. After they saw that I was ok, they gave me my meds and then sent me back to check in . . . and I had to start over from the beginning and wait in all of the same lines again. I counted and it had been over 20 hours straight before I was actually checked in to a cell.

When I finally got sent to my holding cell, I was greeted at the gate by a crazy-looking, tatted-up white dude who reached out to shake my hand. "I'm Mad Dog," he said. "Do you run with the Woods?"

I had no idea what the hell he meant. Woods?

"Whites," he growled. "Are you a white boy?" I said yes, and then he told me to follow him.

This place was packed floor to ceiling with prisoners. It looked like something right out of a movie. There were four giant rows of bunk beds stacked next to one another all the way across the room, leaving a small walking area to get to and from the bathroom between each of them. Mad Dog explained to me that we were in a segregated cell block. There was the whites, or the "Woods" as he called us, then the Mexicans, and finally the "Blacks and Others," which I thought was slightly amusing. I guess all the Asian guys were lumped in as "others" because there weren't enough of them to justify having their own prison gang.

I asked Mad Dog if I was going to be able to make a phone call and see the judge the next day, and he just started laughing. To make it worse he tapped another guy on the shoulder and said: "Hey, our new brother wants to know when he gets to see the judge," and then they both cracked up like it was the funniest thing they'd ever heard. Another guy walking by sneered, "Fuckin' Greenhorn."

I was arrested on a Thursday of a three-day weekend, which apparently is the absolute worst time to be put in LA County. If I was lucky I might be able to see a judge or make a call on Tuesday or Wednesday of the following week. And I had no money on a calling card or anything like that . . . hell, I had no idea how any of this shit even worked.

I figured I better start learning pretty fast because this was shaping up to be my ultimate nightmare. I had a top bunk, which sucked, especially given my heart condition, but I managed to climb up to it. The bunk was all metal and there was a paper-thin plastic thing on top of it to serve as a mattress. Nobody had a pillow, but everyone got a ratty old fuzzy gray blanket no bigger than a beach towel. I saw one poor bastard a few bunks down lying on the fucking metal bunk with nothing because someone had taken his blanket and mattress. Did that make me feel better about my situation? No. All it told me is that things could get even worse.

Around 4 a.m. the guards turned on the lights and started walking through the room banging their batons on the bunks. Why? I had no idea—it just seemed unnecessarily cruel. The guy bunking next to me warned me not to look the police in the eyes and to just keep my head down unless I wanted to get hit with a nightstick. So that's exactly what I did.

By morning I was a nervous wreck. And when I went to get my meds they made me take my entire batch of heart medication for the whole day all at once. One of the pills I was on was called Lasix, and it was a diuretic that made me piss my brains out in order to keep my body from retaining water. I knew that by taking two of them at once, I would be going to the bathroom every five minutes and that was going to be damn near impossible to do under the circumstances.

When I got back to my cell block, Mad Dog was leaving. He had been released, and on his way out the door he told me to check in with this other white guy who would be filling me in on who would be in charge now that he was gone. Before I knew it, this guy was calling for all the Woods to meet in the shower room at the end of the cell block.

I followed the crowd back to the shower area to see what was going on . . . and things just got more surreal. This huge guy who answered to the name of Hill Billy made an announcement about Mad Dog leaving and that he now had seniority in our cell unless there was anyone there who wanted to challenge him to a debate. A debate? Despite it all I almost laughed. What the fuck were they doing, running for president?

This hard-bitten, psycho-looking dude slowly raised his hand. Then another guy stepped in and laid out the terms of the election. "Ok, we have a challenger," he said. "Here is how this works. Hill Billy will have the floor first and then the floor will be turned over to Dirt Bag. They will each make their case for why they should be in charge and we will put it to a vote."

I was in disbelief. Two guys named Dirt Bag and Hill Billy were about to debate each other for prison control and I had to vote for one of them? Me—who just months before would sit around a table with Tobey Maguire and Leo DiCaprio and millionaires and billionaires every week and roast them all for hundreds of thousands of dollars on the turn of a card. Me—who had started a hustle that bust the Hollywood elite wide open. Me—who now having to vote in my new leader was being forced to choose between two white supremacist Neanderthals in a grimy shower block in LA County jail.

Surely, I figured, this was the moment I'd stop falling. Surely this was rock bottom.

Hill Billy made his case first. He was about 6'5" and sported a superlong ZZ Top–style beard. He had a few tattoos including one of those old-fashioned style tats of a ship with the words "Bon Voyage" written beneath it in cursive. For being so big and scary looking, Hill Billy was all about getting along with the Mexicans and the Blacks and Others. He was a bit older than everyone else, and his entire pitch for white leadership revolved around the fact that he just wanted to do his time in peace and wanted us to fall in line with that same philosophy.

When he got done speaking there was a smattering of golf-style claps from the other inmates . . . so I nervously and politely joined in. Then it was Dirt Bag's turn to talk—and he had a much different idea about how things should be run.

Dirt Bag felt that the Woods, short for "peckerwoods" as I would later realize, were being shit on, and he was sick of it. The next time a white guy got called out for something that wasn't his fault, he wanted everyone to rise up and beat the fuck out of whoever the perpetrator was so people would know not to fuck with us.

Jesus Christ. Was this shit really happening? Would I have to dodge a prison race riot over the weekend before even having a chance to make my fucking phone call? Was any of this even real?

As I was still reeling, they called for a vote. "Everybody who votes for Hill Billy raise your hand." I think I was too stunned to raise my hand at first, and before I knew it, I'd missed my chance so I was forced to cast my vote for Dirt Bag instead. The only upside was that while Dirt Bag was far more unstable than Hill Billy, he also happened to stay in the bunk just below me on my left and he looked like just the sort of crazy who might stab you in your sleep or try and rape you in the shower. I figured at least I hadn't antagonized the nutcase.

Thankfully the majority didn't agree with me, and Hill Billy was named the new leader of The Woods. But that wasn't quite the last we heard of Dirt Bag.

When the guards came in for their 4 a.m. shakedown that night, they didn't bother turning on the lights. Instead, four of them headed straight for Dirt Bag's bunk. One of them hit him in the head with his night stick, and the other two dragged him out of bed and began tearing his bunk apart while two others were wailing on him so hard it made the Rodney King beating look like an episode of Sesame Street. Finally, one of the cops reached into his bedroll and pulled out what had to be the largest prison shank of all time.

Forget anything you've seen on TV, this monster had more in common with a fucking Viking Broadsword. It could have killed a man in seconds, and it had been in the hands of a psycho racist lying almost right next to me.

I had to find a way to get the fuck out of that cell block. I couldn't stay there for one more night.

One more crazy thing happened before I left that place. Someone had swiped my breakfast (a tiny cup of Raisin Bran cereal and a small container of room temperature milk) while I had gone to take a piss thanks to all that heart medication, and rather than kick up a fuss about it, I looked around to see if I could find anybody who didn't want their Raisin Bran instead.

Right behind me I hit the jackpot. There was this scared-looking young black kid and he had a deck of cards sitting on his bunk next to his cereal. I quickly asked him if I could show him something with his cards. Finally! Something I knew; finally something I could control.

He agreed and I asked him to pick a card, then told him to put it anywhere in the deck and give it a shuffle. I then took the deck and started turning over cards. I told him that if he saw his card, not to say anything to me. After I had turned over about half the deck, I stopped and said: "I bet you your breakfast that the next card I turn over will be your card!"

He immediately agreed because, of course, I had already turned his card over a long time ago. So instead of flipping the next card in the deck I reached back into the pile and . . . you can guess the rest. It was an obvious trick, but he was a good sport about it, and he gave me his breakfast. His milk was even cold, so that was a bonus.

Five minutes later, I was summoned by Hill Billy for a "sit-down."

"Look," he said, "you're new so I'm gonna cut you a break one time and one time only. Remember when you went to take a piss this morning and left your food on your bunk? Well, we took it from you to teach you a lesson."

I replied, "Sorry, yeah, I shouldn't have left my food alone."

Hill Billy shook his head: "No, that's not the problem. You can leave your food alone and we will always have your back. But you took a piss standing next to a fucking Mexican, and that is not allowed. That's the kinda fuckin' thing that starts wars in this place."

I stammered some kind of apology when he continued: "One more thing, greenhorn. You're not allowed to hustle the Blacks or the Mexicans. If you wanna gamble, stick with your own race from here on out."

I had just been chewed out by the leader of the white prison faction who stole my food because I pissed next to a Mexican guy and hustled a black kid with a card trick in order to eat. I've seen some mad things and had some crazy conversations, but none quite as surreal as this.

Even without a phone call, I knew that Bonnie would have to be working on getting me out of that place . . . and before lunch rolled around I was being called out. Bonnie had arranged it so I could be put somewhere that would reduce my chances of getting into a prison fight. I was trading my blues for a brown jumpsuit and was moved to the health ward, thanks to my heart condition.

Three days of solitary later, I finally got to see my attorney. He told me that Nevada wanted $80,000 just to release me, otherwise they were going to ship me to Vegas in about a month. A month! I would die in there if I had to stay another fucking month. I bit the bullet, got on the phone to some old loan shark buddies of mine, and cut a deal to get me the hell out of there. It still took another two weeks in absolute hell, and being switched to one other cell block way out in the Valley, but finally, I was released. Nevada still had a warrant out for my arrest, but it was no longer nationwide, and I was on my way home for a long hot shower.

How had I ended up in there in the first place? Apparently the asshole with frosted tips that my buddy Jeff made fun of had been so pissed off with me kicking him off my property he had done a nationwide search on me to find the Nevada warrant. He was the one who called it in and had me arrested.

So here I was, a free man again. I had survived being surrounded by rapists, murderers, gangbangers, and white supremacists, and now, surely, I could start again. Not quite.

For a start I no longer had a house to come home to. Everything I owned was gone—repossessed to cover debts or else sold to pay for my attorney's fees.

The IRS had also joined the party and audited me for my 2006 tax return where they decided to disallow all of my losses as a "professional gambler" but accept all of my wins. How convenient for them.

And that wasn't all. I was also being sued. Not by one, or two, but three different companies. I couldn't afford to fight any of it. I couldn't even afford to file bankruptcy at this point.

I had come to LA at the age of eighteen with not much more than the clothes on my back . . . and now, here I was over twenty years later in the exact same boat. Except this time, it didn't seem like such a great adventure. I was homeless. All of my possessions were gone. My wife and kids were 3,000 miles away, and I was living as a charity case in an old friend's guesthouse where his wife grew weed.

I had been on a roller-coaster thrill ride that shot me all the way to the heavens and then took a nosedive into the bowels of hell. The only thing left to do was keel over and die, which I figured would happen very soon.

Two weeks later I was back in the hospital. This time the doctors told me that my heart was functioning at 21 percent and I needed to get my affairs in order because I probably had about five years to live.

My grandmother used to say that God never gives us more than we can handle. I must admit that, right then, finally at my lowest point, I wasn't so sure.

The only person out of the poker crew that I was still talking to was Jon Moonves. I met Jon for lunch one day, and I could barely look him in the eye. And that's when the wisdom of my grandmother became apparent.

Of them all, Moonves showed me what true friendship is all about. Without any discussion of how I would pay him back, he handed me a bank bag with fifteen grand in it. It was enough money to get a few of my things out of pawn and make it back to that small town in the Midwest that I had left when I was a dreamy-eyed eighteen-year-old setting out to conquer the world.

If anything, Jon gave me hope. But that hope started running out soon after I saw how much it was going to cost just to hold on to the few things I had left. The $15k wasn't going to be enough to get me home. I was living in cheap hotels trying to deal with the pawn shops and a storage facility that had changed the lock on my unit for nonpayment.

Finally, when I had absolutely no resources to stay in LA any longer, it was my old friend Dave, one of the guys who moved to California with me when we were kids, who took me in and eventually drove me all the way back to Illinois. Like Moonves, Dave took pity on my ass and loaned me some cash as well. There's a lesson in there somewhere—a lesson that it can be easy to forget when you're raking in millions of dollars with the world's richest and most glamorous people, perhaps.

And now? It's been eight years since the doctors gave me five years to live. Technically I'm on borrowed time . . . had blown up to 299 pounds and added diabetes and clinical depression to my list of ailments.

I've been separated from my wife for over five years now and depend on FaceTime in order to see my daughters on any kind of seminormal basis because I haven't been able to travel due to my poor health or lack of finances. I moved back home to southern Illinois and have been living in my mother's tiny house she bought after having to sell the dream home I had purchased for her when I was on top of the world.

But you know what . . . as I began writing this book, I took some comfort in the fact that I wasn't dead just yet. Would it be possible to lose all the weight, make my heart disease vanish, stop giving myself insulin shots, start my life over in my midforties and regain my fortune, health, and dignity?

Even if it would ultimately be impossible to overcome all the bad beats, I owed it to my two beautiful daughters, Chloe and Callie, to try. Children are an amazing thing. How can you even begin to place a value on such a thing? The moment you hold them for the first time, you know right then and there you would jump in front of a bus in order to keep them from getting hurt. Because of them, as long as I was breathing there may still be a hand to play . . .

EPILOGUE

I did speak to one other person from the big game before I left LA.

During my last days in the city, I got a call from Molly Bloom. She told me of her misadventures in New York and about the book she was writing. Then she began telling me how Tobey was never really my friend, and he only wanted me around because we were able to make money together and how much he bragged about all the dough I was going to make him after our lopsided financial deal the day after my million-dollar disaster.

I sat and listened to her talk. The words washed over me. She told me how even though her book wasn't out yet, she planned on getting a movie deal and how she wanted me to consult on it with her and so on and on.

She wanted to meet me for drinks that weekend at our old stomping ground, the Four Seasons.

The next night, Molly got raided by twenty FBI agents. Her arrest would go on to make headlines across America . . . and so make her book sell even bigger and secure her the film rights she so desperately craved. The next thing I heard was a rumor she was dating Aaron Sorkin.

I haven't spoken to her since. Molly, I will tell you this: I know Tobey will never admit that your book or Sorkin's film got to him, but his career hasn't exactly gone the way he would have liked ever since your little tell-all. He and Jen split up, the movies he's produced haven't done great, he's been blasted in the press . . .

and being portrayed by you, Miss Bloom, as a narcissistic, greedy asshole probably hasn't helped.

Molly, if you are reading this (and I know you are), I would like to remind you that all the guy ever really did to you was make you far richer than you ever deserved to be. I hope it was worth it.

To Tobey I would like to say this. Buddy, I realize our days of hanging out are over. And I guess it might look like my decision to write a tell-all book containing intimate details about your life in a high-stakes gambling ring designed to fleece suckers out of millions of dollars makes me little better than Miss Bloom herself . . .

But my guess is, you understand where I'm coming from. The true story about that time in our lives needed to be told.

And finally, to all of you folks who were kind enough to buy this book, I know there's still one question left hanging over my own head. Given everything that happened, the million-dollar highs, the crazy excess, the fast, beautiful set I ran with, the five-star hotels and model masseuses, the luxury and glamor and sheer golden fucking ecstasy of a sublime hustle perfectly executed . . . would I change anything?

Given losing my house, my cars, getting audited by the IRS, going dead broke, getting sued by multiple people, losing a million dollars in a single night, getting rat-fucked by Ruderman, getting thrown in jail, dying on the table only to be revived and told I only had another five years anyway, having every single thing I owned taken away from me and winding up back in that small town in Illinois I crawled out of two decades before with absolutely nothing left but the clothes on my back . . . would I change anything?

For as long as I can remember, I knew I wanted to be a card sharp.

What do you think?